Liturgy in a Postmodern World

50 More Ways To Use Your Noodle

Loads Of Land and Water Games With Foam Noodle Toys

Chris Cavert
Sam Sikes

Copyright© 2002 by Chris Cavert & Sam Sikes
ISBN 0-9646541-5-6

DoingWorks, Inc.
351 County Road 277
Liberty Hill, TX 78642
(512) 778-6640   fax (512) 778-6640

Printed in the United States of America

Acknowledgments

We want to thank all the noodlers out there. Without your enthusiasm, this book may not have ever materialized.

We also want to thank our courageous friends for giving us there time and smiles for the endless picture sessions. Thanks Bailey, Tori, Matt, Kristin C., Carmen, Steven, C.J., John, Kristin S., Aryn, Katie, Mark, Sandra, Bradley, Emily, Reece, Jackson, Madelyn, Claire, Donna, Kate, Mary, Sara, Sarah, Ken, Todd, and Leigh. A special thanks to our (highly trained) water specialists, Kenya, Bob, and Roger. And thanks to all the parents who gave of their time to get their children to the shoots – we are very grateful!

We'd like to specifically thank the following people (in no particular order) for their game contributions: Karl Rohnke, Mike Spiller, Jim Cain, Chuck Eaton, David Woods, Steve Johnson, Rex Wadsworth, Kip Prichard, Garth Baker, and Rob Benson.

Table of Contents

Introduction

Thanks for picking up, *50 More Ways To Use Your Noodle*. We hope you have a copy of *50 Ways To Use Your Noodle* and are coming back for a second helping. You might have some noodles sitting around somewhere or you've seen them before and wondered, "what the heck could I use those for" (or, you just might have seen the cool cover and wanted to know what was inside). In any case, this book is packed with fun.

50 More Ways to Use Your Noodle, is filled with water and non-water activities, for all ages, that can enhance the gaming potential of teachers, activity directors, program directors, experiential facilitators, parents, and at gatherings of all sorts. The five activity sections of the book include, **Games**, **Problem-Solving, Water Ways, Variations, and Just For Fun**.

The **Games** section contains activities that include running, jumping, dodging, chasing, tagging, ducking, swinging, and diving movements. All necessary for happy healthy bodies. We often use these games as icebreakers and warm-ups to establish a climate of fun. The **Problem-Solving** section is designed within the spirit of Experiential Education - defined by the Association of Experiential Education as, "...a process through which a learner constructs knowledge, skill, and value from direct experience." The activities will encourage players to work together to solve a given problem, often engaging them in areas of pro-social development like teamwork, communication, conflict resolution, leadership, and trust. **Water Ways** is the wet selection of activities designed for water. Unlike most noodle activities in water, these do not involve hitting others or spitting water. The **Variations** section includes activities that are enhancements of activities from the first book or noodle variations of the authors' other books. "**Just For Fun**" is just that!

They are activities to do that make you want to do them more.

We hope this book enriches the lives of those who play and are longing to play. We loved writing this book as much as we have loved playing all the games in it. *50 More Ways To Use Your Noodle* will provide hours of fun over and over again. Use it as a reference and a resource to have fun and make a difference!

The Ingredients For Fun

Noodles come in a wide variety of shapes and colors. The foam toys in this book are by no means all the noodle types the world has to offer. If you see a new noodle you like in the store and it works in the activities, use it!

Below is a list of all the foam noodle types we have utilized in some way to fit the activities in this book.

Maxaroni - A long noodle approximately 62 inches long and 3 inches in diameter

1 Maxaroni = 2 Midaronis or approximately 21 Minironis

Midaroni - Half of a Maxaroni

Minironi - A Maxaroni piece 3 inches long

Meatball - A 1 1/4 inch long Maxaroni Rex

Maxaroni Rex - A noodle approximately 58 inches long and 4 inches in diameter. Use this type of noodle for the meatballs and a caber toss or two.

1 Maxaroni Rex = approximately 46 meatballs

The ideal number of props for groups of up to 30 players:
- 30 Midaronis
- 100 Minironis
- 100 Meatballs
- 4 Maxaronis

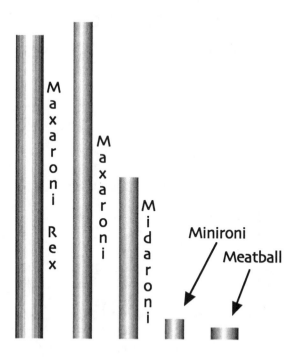

Maxaroni Rex

Maxaroni

Midaroni

Minironi

Meatball

Other materials you may want for some of the activities:

• <u>Bandannas</u> - used as blindfolds

• <u>Spot Markers</u> - usually rubber or carpet pieces used to mark the location of a player, often meatballs can be used in place of "spots"

• <u>Ropes</u> - a bright colored rope to mark boundaries

• <u>Masking Tape</u> - regular or blue masking tape is strong enough to hold noodles together, but weak enough not to rip the foam

• <u>Hula-Hoops</u> - not to hula, but for boundary markers

Cutting your noodle
and other important noodle properties

You may have to cut your noodle to fit the game needs in this book, read the following pages carefully.

What you will need to cut your noodle:
- An adult
- A serrated bread knife or electric knife
- A measuring tape
- A cutting board
- A non-permanent marker

Step 1) This cutting job can be dangerous. Sharp knives cut more than foam. Be careful!

** The best way to cut your own minironis and meatballs is to make a noodle cutter as described three pages after this one. If you don't make one, just follow the remaining steps.

** The best way to cut a midaroni is to balance a maxaroni on the edge of your serrated knife. As long as you have removed any stickers, the balance point will be the center of the noodle. Just cut where the balance point is.

Step 2) Measure your noodle and mark it with a dot or small line where you want to cut it. Meatballs are 1.25 inches thick and minironis are three inches long. Midaronis are half the length of a long noodle or "maxaroni."

Step 3) Place a cutting board under your noodle before performing the noodlectomy. Failure to use a cutting board results in a sliced carpet or linoleum and a dull knife too.

Step 4) Hold the knife straight to make a perfect cut. Carefully cut through the noodle where you marked it. Continue the steps above until you finish cutting.

Step 5) Put your cutting materials away. Celebrate! It's time to play!

Other noodle properties (or The noodle howevers):
Noodles are surprisingly durable. People can stand on them. <u>However</u>, it is best if they remove their shoes first.

Noodles can be glued together with hot glue. <u>However</u>, they will melt if the glue is too hot. Squirt some in the middle and then weld the seam. Hold the pieces together longer than usual because the foam is a heat insulator and takes longer to cool. Pliable craft glue works well too.

Noodles float in water, <u>however</u>, don't dry them by the fire or in the microwave.

Noodles look and feel great, <u>however</u>, don't try to eat one because it will give you a bad stomachache (not to say that any stomachaches are good).

Have fun!!

Disclaimer

All active games contain some inherent risk of injury. The authors have devoted reasonable attention to the safety of any activity included within this book by describing potential hazards and playing the games themselves and with others.

The reader assumes all risk and liability for any loss or damage that may result from the use of the materials contained in this book. Liability for any claim, whether based upon errors or omissions in this book shall be limited to the purchase price of this book.

Whew! Now that that's said . . . **LET'S PLAY!**

Noodle Cutter

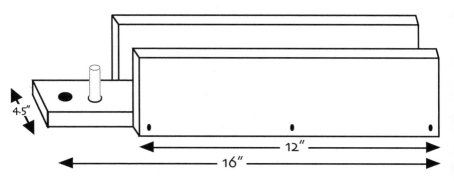

The noodle cutter is something we have used since the first Noodle book to cut our noodles and fill orders for people who didn't want to cut them. Sam still has his original cutter. It is made of wood screwed together. There are two holes drilled for a small dowel rod. The dowel rod acts as a stop for the noodle so that the cut will be at either 1 1/4 inches for meatballs or 3 inches for minironis.

Since we published the first Noodle book in 1997, we have heard many methods of cutting the noodles including some of the following: band saw, deli-meat cutter, hot wire, hacksaw, and paper cutter. Below are the materials and instructions for building a simple and effective noodle cutter:

RAW MATERIALS:
- 1 - 1" x 6" x 3' 4" Board - Cut into two one-foot boards. The remaining 16" board; rip to 4.5 inches wide.
- 6 - 2" Deck screws
- 1 - 3/8" x 2" Dowel rod
- 1 Serrated bread knife - The longer the blade, the easier the cutting will be.

INSTRUCTIONS:

Saw the 1 X 6 board into three pieces: two 12-inch pieces and one 16-inch piece. Saw the 16-inch board lengthwise to make it 4.5 inches wide.

Saw a dowel two inches long. Screw together the boards as shown in the diagram. Drill two holes halfway through the baseboard 3-inches and 1.25-inches from the left edge of the upright boards so that the holes will support the dowel rod to act as a stop for the noodle.

To cut a minironi, slide a maxaroni into the channel so that the end stops at 3-inches because of the dowel rod. Use the left edges of the upright boards as a straightedge and saw through the noodle. When you lift the knife, the minironi will likely lift out so you can push the long noodle to the stop again for another cut. Continue carefully until you have all the minironis you need. For meatballs the procedure is the same except that the dowel is moved to the 1.25-inch distance and you cut a maxaroni rex (4-inch in diameter noodle).

Testing

TEST: **Bend to Break** - We bent a midaroni both ways in the middle so that the ends touched on each bend.
RESULTS: On average, there were 202 bends before the noodle broke in half.

TEST: **Chlorine Test** - We placed a slice of noodle in a glass jar containing a concentrated chlorine solution and left it in overnight. We left another slice of the same noodle in a dresser drawer overnight.
RESULTS: Both noodles looked and felt the same (aside from one being wet). The slice from the jar maintained a strong chlorine odor for at least a day or two.

TEST: **Sun Test** - We placed a midaroni in the back window of a 1991 Ford Escort Wagon for 14 months. The other half of the maxaroni was placed in Sam's closet.
RESULTS: The noodle exposed to the sun looked remarkably similar to the one from Sam's closet. However, when someone gripped the sun baked noodle it left half-inch indentations to matched their fingers. The handprints lasted for 10 minutes. There was a solid core that seemed unaffected by the sun's rays. Apparently the sun deteriorates the plastic to the point that the air bubbles break.

TEST: **Carpet Test** - Chris loaned several noodles to an indoor training facility with carpet on the floor. The noodles were at least 2 years old and had been used in several training sessions with both kids and adults. They still looked great when they arrived at the facility.
RESULTS: After 2 months in the facility, the noodles looked extremely worn on the outside layer. They were "fuzzed." It was much like the two sides to leather; they looked like the smooth side when they started and then they looked and felt like the rough suede side 2 months later.

TEST: **Pressure Test** - We parked a car on a minironi for ten days.
RESULTS: The noodle was flattened and showed a clear tread mark. The noodle did not resume its original shape, but stayed approximately half an inch thick.

TEST: **30-Mile Drag Test** - We dragged a midaroni by a short length of rope behind Sam's Toyota van.
RESULTS: The noodle had a rounded end where the rope was tied to it. The other end was rounded and tapered like the point of a pencil. Overall the noodle was very dirty (black and grey instead of red). You can get similar results without the dirt if you use a belt sander.

Strobe

The following letter is a great example of creativity under pressure. Sam received it in an e-mail. Hopefully it will be helpful in your facilitating future.

Sam,

It was 10 PM on the second night of a retreat, the weather was cold and wet outside, they were Junior Highers, I was alone, and they were getting restless. It's a scene that could paralyze most people allowing the anarchy of pubescence hormones run amuck. But, I had a secret weapon!

A strobe light!

We played noodle games by the on again, off again rhythms of an inexpensive Radio Shack strobe light.

Two hours later, they were satisfied and very tired, making control a non-issue.

Trust Run and the one where you try to knock the circle off the other's head (we played for the championship of the world) were the favorites.

Of course, it is important to make sure that strobe lights don't trigger seizures in any of the participants.

Just a new twist on what is becoming a camp favorite.

Blessings,

Chuck Eaton

! Games !

The Games to follow are intended to promote cooperative fun and fierce-less competition (the sort of competition where all players are having fun and are not being beaten-up by negative put-downs).

When you're getting ready to play, please consider a few things. Make sure your group is ready, both mentally and physically, for the games you are going to present. If you have a concern about the way your group will handle the noodle equipment, you might want to consider doing some other games that do not require equipment. This will give you an opportunity to observe the group's playing interaction. If you use the noodles and the group is being unsafe, please stop the activity and try something a little less threatening. If they are playing well, continue what you are facilitating or progress to more complex activities.

Make sure your group is physically ready by starting with low-level movement games, followed by some stretching, and then progress into some higher-level movement games. Those underused muscles tend to get noticed during the fun noodle encounters -- use your best judgment when developing your progression of activities.

One last thought we would like to share. End the games when the players are still having fun. When you do this, groups are more likely to want to play them again in the future. This leaves your bag of games always overflowing with options.

Off With Their Hats

GROUP SIZE:
Pairs

TIME:
10-45 minutes

PROPS:
• 6 Midaronis per pair
• 2 Foam connectors or 2 flip chart markers

OBJECTIVE:
Knock the hat off your opponent first.

HISTORY:
This activity was developed from a brainstorming session after a noodle workshop in 1997. It is one of those fun games for those who like competition.

PREPARATION:
You will need to make two hats. Connect two midaronis into circles so that they form two hats. The foam connectors that look like collars work well, but can be difficult to find. Another method for making each noodle hat is to use a midaroni made with a hole through it. Push a magic marker halfway into one end of the noodle, and then join the other end to make a circle. Sometimes a little masking tape is needed to keep the noodle ends together. I would suggest using blue masking tape because it will not damage the noodle.

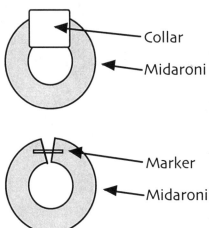

INSTRUCTIONS:
This match will be played in a best three out of five rounds. You each should place a foam hat on your head so that it would fall off if you bowed forward. (No pulling it down around your ears or holding the

hat on your head during play.) Each of you will also hold two noodles for offense and defense.

You both should face each other and walk together close enough to touch noodles. When you are ready, clap your own noodles together once at the same time as your opponent and begin.

To win a round, you must use your noodles to knock your opponent's hat off his head. If both hats are knocked off at the same time, the last hat to touch the floor wins that round.

LEADER NOTES:
This seems like a game that should need helmets or some protective gear for the players. In truth, the pairs don't get a chance to swing hard because they will leave themselves vulnerable or will jostle off their own hat. Each person stays in a high-speed offensive and defensive posture.

It is important that this activity is done only in pairs. Involving more players at the same time does put people at risk of being hurt by an unexpected hard swat to the head. Watching out for one other player is enough of a challenge.

Dressed to Play

Bumper Cars

GROUP SIZE:
15 to 30 players

TIME:
10 to 15 minutes

PROPS:
- 1 Midaroni and 1 blindfold for each player (you can also ask players to just close their eyes).
- Something to mark the corners of the boundary area – we suggest something flat so players cannot trip over them. (The boundary markers will only be for the facilitator(s) who are monitoring the activity – since everyone else is blindfolded and can't see the boundaries anyway. But you knew that.)

OBJECTIVES:
Practice using the Noodle Bumper by going out into the crowd of bumpers feeling safe with the process.

HISTORY:
In the Adventure Based Activity field, we do many games that are set up using the "Bumpers Up" position. Most of the games involve blindfolds or closing the eyes – which fits into activities involving trust building. "Bumpers Up" is players putting up their hands and arms about chest high, a slight bend in the elbows, palms open, with fingers pointing up. This position helps to cushion most contact between blinded players. So, we thought, "Why not use a noodle?"

PREPARATION:
Teach the Noodle Bumper position. Hold each end of a midaroni – one end in each hand - about bellybutton level out in front of you, elbows at your sides. Create a slight bend in the noodle so the rounded bend points out away from you – for your bumper.

INSTRUCTIONS:
Have all the players stand outside of the boundary area and place their blindfolds on their eyes (or have them close their eyes). Before entering the boundary area, have the players get into the Noodle Bumper

position. When each player is ready, she can enter the boundary area for some bumping action. We only allow walking during Bumper Cars – most players do this naturally when they cannot see, however, we have had some of those daredevils who like to go fast no matter what. When a player bumps another, there should be a slight stop, then a small turn in either direction, then continue in the forward direction. Ask the players not to move backwards during the activity.

We also like to promote some car noises for extra fun. How about some motor noises when moving? Then there is the "Errrrrk" sound when a player bumps into someone. There's also the natural "Ohhh" when a player is bumped into. And of course there are all sorts of other noises that show up.

LEADER NOTES:
It will be your job to watch the sidelines for stray cars. If possible have another facilitator available to help. If a player starts wandering outside of the boundary area, just carefully steer them back into the pile – most players move back towards the noise on their own, but it's good to be there just in case.

VARIATIONS:
Use the noodle bumpers for other activities you might know that call for "Bumpers Up."

Rope Circle Tag

GROUP SIZE:
10 to 15 players per rope circle.

TIME:
15 to 20 minutes.

PROPS:
- 2 to 4 midaronis
- An activity rope 30 to 50 feet long. You will want at least 3 feet of rope room for each player.

OBJECTIVES:
A player, or players, in the center of the rope circle try to get out of the center by tagging the hands of the players who are holding onto the rope.

HISTORY:
The cowboys played this game way back in the 1800s after a long day on the trail moving cattle. After supper, they would round up with a rope and a couple of shovels. An old can was tossed out into the desert. The first two cowboys to shoot a hole in the can got to start in the middle. You really wanted to

start in the middle because being hit with that shovel was no day at the beach.

PREPARATION:
You'll want to tie a good knot with the ends of the rope so you have a circle to hold onto. A square knot works well (left over right, then right over left). A Bowline would be better (the dragon comes out of the pond, swoops down and under to pick up the princess then goes back into the pond). The Fisherman's knot works well as well (you'll have to look this one up).

SCENARIO:
You (and some friends) are trapped in the circle of myrrh. There are doors everywhere but the handles to these doors are constantly moving. To make things even more difficult, each door has two handles. You have with you a special key to open any door for your escape. Once you hit a handle with your key, the door is half-open. If you are successful in hitting a handle of a door that is half-open, it opens completely and you are freed from the circle.

INSTRUCTIONS:
Circle up all players and have them hold onto the rope circle with both hands about waist high using an overhand grasp. Choose 2 or 3 players to go into the center of the circle. Give each of the center players one midaroni. When the game starts, the center players try to hit the hands of the players holding onto the rope.

Rope holders can slide their hands on the rope but cannot let go. If they let go, that hand cannot be placed back on the rope. When a hand is hit by the midaroni, that hand is removed from the rope. When the second hand is hit that hand is removed from the rope and this player then takes the place of the midaroni wielding center player who dealt the second-hand-elimination-blow. (If you lose both hands you're in the middle.)

Center players can go for a hit on any hand. However, once they make an attempt or successful hit on a rope holder (let's say player A), the center player must make a play on another circle player before making another play on player A. For sporting reasons we don't allow a center player to just stand in front of one player and take whacks at him until he is out. Also, as another sporting rule, it is not allowed to take alternate whacks at players standing next to each other. So, center players should move around to different parts of the circle to catch circle players off guard. When a center player hits the last remaining hand of a circle player, the two switch positions.

Hands are never returned to the rope during the game unless you are a center player taking a position on the rope.

LEADER NOTES:
You might need to state a caution to the circle players about standing too close to the rope. Noodles may come in contact with other parts of the body if one is standing too close to the rope - if you know what we mean!

Some facilitators prefer to use a noodle approximately 1 foot long for each whacker. The shorter noodle allows the rope circle to be smaller and it gives the rope holders more of a chance to escape the hits.

Full Contact Golf

GROUP SIZE:
2 to 5 players for each course

TIME:
30 minutes

PROPS:
- 1 Midaroni for each player
- 1 Minironi or meatball for each player - Each noodle should be a different color.

OBJECTIVES:
Knock a noodle to predetermined targets in the least number of strokes.

HISTORY:
Jim Cain first reported this activity to us. He said some boys had created the game to pass the time. The fun happened when a player missed his ball on a swing. Read below for the details.

PREPARATION:
Decide what "holes" define the course. The course is similar to a Frisbee golf course. Locate objects that need to be hit to designate each hole. An example of a hole might be a door, pole, tree, or backpack. A course may have anywhere from 4 to 18 "holes" depending on the length of time you have to play.

SCENARIO:
You are all professional golfers of the future. The game has changed greatly in the past 200 years. Because of the anger and frustration associated with the sport, the clubs and balls have been replaced with foam balls and clubs. Also, because of environmental pressures associated with putting holes in the ground, the sport is now played by hitting the ball to a preexisting landmark so that the hole is complete when your ball contacts the landmark. One other change is what happens when a player misses the ball during a stroke. The opposing players all yell, "Wiff!" and hit the player with their clubs for a few seconds before continuing to play. Scoring remains the same.

INSTRUCTIONS:
Players will take turns hitting their own minironi (ball) until the ball hits the "hole."

Players stand at a specific place on the ground to tee off toward the predetermined landmark. A player can tee off by leaving the minironi on the ground or tossing it straight up in the air and swinging his club like a bat. A player may only pick up his ball when teeing off and after completing a hole.

Each time a player swings the club to hit his minironi it counts as a stroke. Even though the minironi may move as the club swings past it, if no physical contact is made it is declared a missed swing, nevertheless the attempted swing is still counted as a stroke. A missed swing should be followed closely by the opposing players hitting the player who missed the shot with their noodles and yelling, "Wiff."

When a player finally hits the hole with his minironi, he picks up his ball and waits while the rest of the players take turns to "hole out." Play begins again with the players taking turns to tee off near the completed hole.

As the holes are completed the scores should be recorded and totaled at the last hole of the course.

The player with the least number of strokes by the end of the game wins.

More rules may be added if all the players agree. Other rules might include: a penalty stroke if your minironi goes to a place that cannot be hit, a dog grabs your ball and runs away, wind blows your minironi away, etc.

LEADER NOTES:
The game can be played so that everyone is against everyone. You can also make it a team activity keeping a team score for players on the same team with each team having the same ball. If you have several groups of players, you can have a contest for the lowest group score even though each player still has his own ball.

Do be prepared to intervene with kids when it comes to "Wiffs." Some kids (big and small) have a hard time knowing when to stop hitting.

Caber Tossing

GROUP SIZE:
2 - 10 players

TIME:
10-15 minutes per game

PROPS:
- 1 Maxaroni <u>or</u> 2 midaronis connected together <u>or</u> 1 maxaroni rex approximately 5 feet long
- Masking tape (blue masking tape makes the marks easier to see)

OBJECTIVE:
Toss a noodle so that it lands in the 12 o'clock position and on the box to maximize points. Younger players can learn to tell time on an analog clock and use negative numbers.

HISTORY:
The Scottish game of caber tossing has been around for centuries. A participant tosses the equivalent of a 16 to 20 foot telephone pole with the small end in his hands so that the larger end hits the ground causing the smaller end to rotate over and land farthest away from him. The goal is to flip the log so that it lands as close the 12 o'clock position as possible.

This noodle game was originally developed using the larger diameter noodles. It is not much of a strength challenge as it is a technique challenge. The regular full-length noodle (maxaroni) is the most challenging.

SCENARIO:
The year is 1291 in Scotland. Rather than fight, you and several others, including William Wallace, decide to hold a contest of skill. Each player must toss a caber in the air so that it rotates and lands straight. Whoever has the best skills and luck after three tosses wins.

PREPARATION:
Using the masking tape, mark a tossing line, a distance line, a 1-foot square, clock times, and the 12 o'clock line as shown below. Make a tape ring around one end of your "caber."

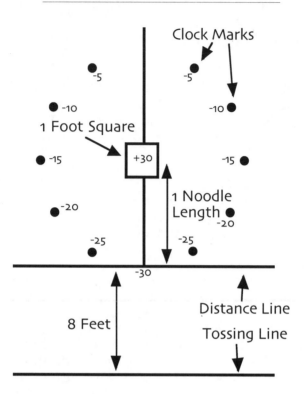

INSTRUCTIONS:

Stand behind the tossing line. Hold the noodle in both of your palms by the end without the tape ring. Toss the noodle so that the taped end hits the floor beyond the distance line.

The best throw will land in the 12 o'clock position and land across the box at the same time.

<u>Scoring:</u> The one-foot square is worth 30 points if the noodle lands and stays anywhere over it. The clock marks represent negative points in 5-point increments from 12 o'clock. For example, if the noodle lands closest to the 1 o'clock or 11 o'clock position and on top of the box, 5 points are subtracted from the 30 to leave 25 points for that toss. If the noodle lands at the 6 o'clock position and not on the box, the score is a negative 30 (the lowest

score possible). If the toss lands shorter than the distance line or lands on the untaped end first, the toss gets no score. See the examples below.

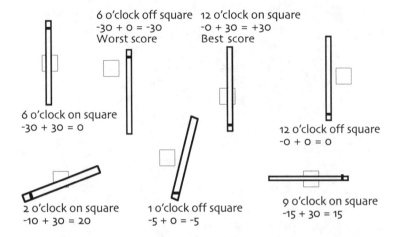

6 o'clock off square
-30 + 0 = -30
Worst score

12 o'clock on square
-0 + 30 = +30
Best score

6 o'clock on square
-30 + 30 = 0

12 o'clock off square
-0 + 0 = 0

2 o'clock on square
-10 + 30 = 20

1 o'clock off square
-5 + 0 = -5

9 o'clock on square
-15 + 30 = 15

In order to assess "what time it is," a scorekeeper may need to move the noodle (keeping it at the same angle) so that the taped end is in the middle of the square box. The clock position that the untaped end is closest to determines how many points to subtract.

After three rounds and each person has made three tosses, the best toss wins. If there is a tie, do you have to go for a "flip off"? I think not!

LEADER NOTES:
This game is harder than it looks. Encourage different strategies to make the best score.

Ceiling height has made little difference in the game. You can certainly play indoors with 8-foot ceilings or outside with no ceilings.

Noodle Drumming

GROUP SIZE:
Any

TIME:
1 - 30 minutes

PROPS:
- Any of the noodles for each person. All can make their own "music."

OBJECTIVES:
Make music through a variety of rhythms and sounds using noodles.

HISTORY:
After writing the first noodle book, we noticed how people really liked to whack those noodles on the floor. We needed a good way to lead a group into action without causing people to call the cops. (The noodles randomly hit on the ground do sound like gunfire.) Drumming has been a great way to "create a space" for a group through rhythm.

PREPARATION:
Organize your noodles by section if you desire. It is ideal to have two minironis or meatballs per player. One midaroni per person works well also.

SCENARIO:
You and your mission team have been working hard all day building homes deep in the rainforest. As customary, you all are asked to join in a celebration of rhythm and sound. You're not sure what to do with the instrument they gave you, but they said you would figure out what to do. All you know is that you are supposed to start quietly, build in energy and volume and then slowly become quiet again until the leader signals a stop.

INSTRUCTIONS:
Drumming with the noodles can be anything from a spontaneous event of noise and energy that lasts a minute or two to an organized "symphony" of foam that can be practiced and presented.

A "magic" and "cool" aspect of drumming is that order develops out of chaos. You never know what rhythms and songs will eventually occur. At first it is typically a lot of disjointed noise, but it will grow into its own structure.

If you find yourself in the midst of a spontaneous noodle drumming session, take a lead role. Go with the energy of the group and then bring it to a close quickly if needed or extend it if you want.

For a more organized variety, demonstrate examples of making the various sounds. Establish a way of stopping the drumming. Encourage people to discover the natural rhythms their instruments will play as they start. Then play!

An example of a drumming stop is to countdown from five to the beat. When you get to one, lift your instruments into the air.

Common sounds:
Midaronis
- Whack the noodle on the floor, leg, or other midaroni - sharp and loud sound
- Rub the ends together - sounds like rubbing two pieces of toast together (only no mess).
- Bounce an end on the floor - deeper bass sound
- Rub the side - longer rustling sound
- Swing it quickly through the air - low whoosh sound

Minironis and/or meatballs -
- Rub two together - sounds like rubbing two pieces of toast together (still, no mess).
- Clap two together - sharp quick sound
- Beat on one or two on the floor like drums - dull thuds
- Pluck one with your thumb - sharp popping sound

LEADER NOTES:
This activity can be very noisy. Be a good neighbor to anyone in nearby rooms.

Noodle Darts/Soup

GROUP SIZE:
Teams of 2 to 3 players play other teams of 2 to 3 players. Several games can be going on at one time.

TIME:
10 to 15 minutes per game. Allow for more time if the teams want to play the best of five.

PROPS:
- Different colored midaronis for each team - Each player on each team has his or her own midaroni.
- Hula Hoops or rope circles about 3 feet in diameter (If you're playing at the beach you could draw a circle in the sand.)

OBJECTIVES:
Teams try to be the first to score points to win this game.

HISTORY:
Lawn darts were a favorite past time of ours back in the 70s and 80s. Well we all know what happened there. After some litigation, the real Lawn Darts are no more. So, we thought we would jump on the bandwagon of Lawn Dart supplements.

PREPARATION:
Set out the hula-hoops or rope circles about 15 to 20 feet apart. You're ready to go.

INSTRUCTIONS:
Both teams take a position behind one of the hoops for the first throw. Flip to see what team will start. Teams take turns throwing/tossing a midaroni towards the far hoop. Score as follows:

2 Points - most noodle in the hoop/soup
1 Point - next most noodle in the hoop/soup or closest to the hoop/soup

If a midaroni is lying on top of another midaroni the bottom midaroni is canceled out.

A game to 15 points is often a good round. Playing the best of five continues the excitement.

The team with the highest score at the time is the

first team to throw back the other way.

VARIATIONS:
To give a bit more direct action to the noodles, add a four-inch wooden dowel section to one end of the noodle - you'll need the noodles with the holes in the center. Remember to take the wooden dowels out when playing other noodle games.

NOTES:

_____

_____

_____

_____

_____

_____

_____

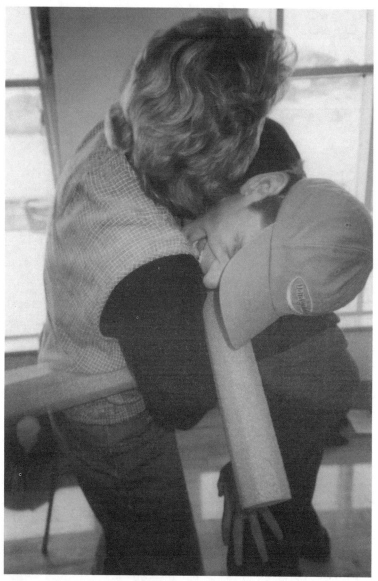

Parts Passing

Parts Passing

GROUP SIZE:
10 to 50 players (if you have room to make a circle that big)

TIME:
10 to 20 minutes depending on the size of the circle

PROPS:
• 3 Different colored midaronis for every six players

OBJECTIVES:
To have fun and break the ice while passing noodles around the circle using different parts of the body.

HISTORY:
Passing the orange around with a chin pinch has been done since, well, since the first orange we think. Why not add another food group?

INSTRUCTIONS:
Ask your group to make a comfortable size circle facing in towards the center. Here's the big picture. The players will be passing around the midaroni using different parts of their bodies. First they will be passing one color around up under their armpits. Then, they pass a different colored noodle between their knees. The final color is passed around squeezed under the chin and chest. By the end, all of these passes will be happening at the same time.

Setting this up will depend on the size of your group. If you have a large group you can start with more noodles. Here's a small group example; let's say we have 12 participants in our group. We will give one, let's say orange, midaroni to each player at the 12, and 6, o'clock positions and ask them to put the stick up under their armpit and then pass these around to the right - armpit passing only. After a few passes we'll stop the group (hold onto those pit sticks), and then hand out two more, let's say yellow, noodles to some players who don't have a noodle stuck in their arm pit at the moment. These midaronis go in the knee-squeeze position and are passed around to the left. Ready go - both armpits (to the right) and knee passing (to the left). Stop the group after several of these noodle exchanges and add in two chin passes to the right using purple noodles (my favorites). All the passes go on simultaneously for a while. Stop the action while there is still laughter. (This activity provides numerous photo opportunities!)

LEADER NOTES:
The use of hands is optional. We will allow the players to adjust the noodles if they need to. Also, squelch any sexual joking, letting the children know that it is unacceptable in your program - then move right on.

VARIATIONS:
Well, if you have some oranges around - why not?

Pick Up the Pasta

GROUP SIZE:
2 to 5 players per game work out well

TIME:
10 to 20 minutes

PROPS:
• 15 to 30 Midaronis total - three different colors

OBJECTIVES:
Score points by picking up midaronis without disturbing other midaronis. The player with the most points after all midaronis are picked up wins the game.

HISTORY:
Pick-Up the Pasta is a macro variation of Pick-Up Sticks - which is a variation of the game Spellicans that originated in China.

PREPARATION:
You will want to prepare your noodle count before getting started. Let's say we have Red, Yellow and Purple noodles. Here's what we found works the best: For two players use 15 midaronis - 3 of each color. For three players use 18 midaronis - 6 of each color. For four or five players use 24 midaronis - 8 of each color.

INSTRUCTIONS:
Determine an order of play - be creative. The last player in the order gets to perform the "drop." Drop the noodles by gathering all of them in one big hug, holding them towards the bottom of the vertical pile, and then dropping them to the floor. (If the amount of noodles supersedes the arm capacity of the dropper, then two successive drops can be done - the second right on top of the first). This drop should leave the noodles in somewhat of a pile (As the facilitator, you might find the need to challenge the group by putting some of the lone noodles into the pile).

With the pile in place, the game plays as follows. Inform the players that each colored noodle will be worth a certain point value. For instance, the Reds are worth 1 point, Yellows 2 points, and Purples 3 points. Each player in turn attempts to remove one of the noodles without disturbing any of the other noodles. Once a player has touched one of the noodles he is not allowed to touch another noodle during that turn - you must play the first noodle touched. If the player successfully separates the noodle from the pile, without moving any of the other noodles, he keeps this noodle and the points it is worth. If a player, while trying to remove a noodle, disturbs another noodle in the pile (someone in the group notices another noodle move), he must let go of the noodle he is touching, letting fall back into the pile.

After each attempt, successful or not, the next player takes his turn. Once all the noodles are gone from the pile, the game is over. Players count their points to determine a winner for the game.

LEADER NOTES:
The judging on the "noodle movement" can be a sensitive issue for some groups. However, how can groups work together to create the well-played game? Be ready for arbitration if needed.

The round noodles do roll more than the other shapes. Feel free to have the group bend the noodles before starting the game or just use the non-round noodles if there is a problem.

VARIATIONS:
One of our favorite "get to know you" variations is to assign a question category to each color. When someone picks off a noodle out of the pile they get a question from the category. For example, the Red noodles go with a Favorites category. The Yellow noodles might be a family category. The Purples could be Television. Create a question list before hand so you're ready to query.

Parco Molo

GROUP SIZE:
10 to 20 players

TIME:
15 to 25 minutes

PROPS:
• 1 Midaroni and one blindfold for every 6 players
• 4 Cones or noodles to mark off the boundaries if you are not playing on a lined surface

OBJECTIVES:
While blindfolded and armed with a noodle, try to first find, and then tag other players in the game

33

who are not blindfolded.

HISTORY:
We first played this activity with David Woods, under a different name (I'll bet you can figure out the name), at the 2001 National Challenge Course Symposium. He was having great success with it and we've been having fun with Parco Molo ever since.

PREPARATION:
Create an appropriate size boundary for the size of your group. Let's say if you have a group of 10, a good size might be about 20 by 20-foot square. The more players you have the bigger you want the boundary area.

You will also want to present the blindfolded player's role and actions. When a player is blindfolded she will be using a noodle to tag other players. This blindfolded player will want to keep the free arm and hand up in the air in the "bumpers up" position to prevent her from bumping onto other players during the game. Also, when using the noodle for tagging, all swings must be in the horizontal direction at or below waste level. Whenever possible we like to give everyone a noodle and have them practice this tagging motion with their eyes closed so they can get the feel for it. This practice seems to cut down on the uppercut swings that can clip chins.

INSTRUCTIONS:
If you know the pool game relative of this one you have a head start. This is how we play the land version. Let's say we have 12 players in our game. Choose two players to be the blindfolded taggers to start the game. After donning their eye wear, each tagger is given a midaroni. All other players in the game, the sighted ones, can move about within the boundary area while the taggers are being blindfolded. The game begins when one of the taggers yells, "Parco!" At this first call, all the sighted players must stop moving (or "freeze" if this is a better word) and say, "Molo" in a nice strong voice.

The game is now on. From this point the taggers have 2 minutes to try to tag as many of the sighted players with their noodles as possible. Sighted players are allowed to use three steps (one leg moving in any direction) at any time during the game. The taggers have 10 "Parcos" to use during the game (it's nice to have a facilitator help keep track of the Parcos). Hopefully the two taggers in this game will work together on the Parco calls so they don't waist them - nothing like a little teamwork to spice things up a bit.

As the game moves on it is most likely that some sighted players will be tagged - any noodle tags on any part of the body are counted. (We do make a clear warning to the sighted players to protect their head as much as possible. If the sighted players choose to squat down there is more chance of a head shot, so be warned!) Once a sighted player is tagged, he must stand up at the tagged point and become a "beeper post" - self protected stationary objects used as obstacles for increased adventure. These frozen beeper posts are silent until a tagging player moves within 3 feet of them. If a tagger breaks the 3-foot plane, the beeper post sends out a continuous warning until the tagger leaves the 3-foot area. This warning sounds like, "beep, beep, beep, beep, beep...", and so on. Most beeper post warnings get louder and faster the closer the tagger gets, but this is not a requirement.

So as the game is going, you will see blindfolded taggers slowly making their way through a maze of beeping bodies who are constantly protecting vital areas of their person from misguided noodle strikes. You will also see sighted players strategically positioning themselves around the playing area to avoid being found by the foam. All in all this is a fun game to watch as well as play.

After the two minutes are up, count the number of beeper posts for that pair's total score. Bring on another pair for the next game.

LEADER NOTES:

It will be important to keep an eye on the blindfolded players so they do not travel out of bounds too long. You will also be taking for granted that all the sighted players will have the integrity to take no more than three steps during the game.

VARIATIONS:

This is also a great summer weather game. What if the blindfolded players are armed with a cup of water used for tagging? Each tagger will need a water re-loader or bucket of water for this variation.

NOTES:

_____

_____

_____

_____

_____

_____

_____

William Tell

GROUP SIZE:
Multiple groups of 3-player teams play against the clock. Any number of teams can play.

TIME:
10 to 15 minutes

PROPS:
• 3 Midaronis and one hula-hoop for each team

- Something to mark the shooting point and target point like rope lines, chalk, tape or cones

OBJECTIVES:
Throw as many midaroni arrows through the hula-hoop target within a predetermined time, taking three rounds per game.

HISTORY:
This is another fun activity shared by David Woods. We have found it to be a great way to develop small team strategies and help introduce the concept of personal bests as compared to the competition this game seems to promote.

PREPARATION:
You will want to set up the archery ranges before play begins. Each team will need a shooting line and a target point. The distance between the two will depend on the toss-ability of the group members you are working with. The closer the lines are together the easier it is. A pretty good rule of thumb is a distance of about 1 foot per year of age; however, a distance of over 15 feet apart is fairly difficult.

INSTRUCTIONS:
When all the ranges are prepared, each team will have to decide a shooting order. There are three roles in each round. The shooter stands behind the shooting line and tosses the midaronis toward the target hoping to get the noodle through the hula-hoop. The target player holds the hula-hoop on top of his head like a big apple (hence the name from the famous story) with the opening toward the shooter. The hula hoop must be touching the head of the target player at all times during each round; however, the target player can move anywhere behind the target point in an attempt to increase the odds of the noodle going through the target. Finally, the retriever is the player who returns the arrows to the shooter - by any means possible. If time is available we like to give the teams a little practice before they choose an order and the game begins.

There are three rounds in each game and players rotate roles after each round - shooter to target, target to retriever, retriever to shooter. When the time starts, the shooter tries to toss the midaroni arrows through the hula-hoop target. The shooter must stay behind the shooting line and the target must stay behind the target point. The retriever is allowed to move anywhere between and around his teammates in order to get the noodle arrows back to the shooter. Each round lasts one minute with 30 seconds of planning time before each round. At no time can any player disturb the path of any arrow or player from another team.

After three rounds find out the scores of each team and challenge them to beat that score after playing another game. Give them a minute to plan and then start the next game.

LEADER NOTES:
Whatever way you play this game - head to head, or personal best score, emphasize the components of the game like problem solving, team roles and responsibilities, and sportsmanship. Competition helps to fuel motivation. How we treat each other within the competitive arena is an important seed to sow.

VARIATIONS:
What about blindfolding the target? That sounds like fun. But you might want to have helmets!? No, we've got it. Have the target player turn and face away from the shooter. That would save a little face (pun?).

Spear the Whale

GROUP SIZE:
4 to 8 players

TIME:
10 to 20 minutes (when you play a best of 5)

PROPS:
- A small gauge metal or rubber ring with at least a 4-inch diameter (no bigger than 5 inches). You can find these at most craft stores (You can also fashion a ring with a wire coat hanger if you have a few tools.).
- Approximately 6 feet of string for each ring
- 1 Midaroni for every player - different colors for each team.
- 1 Spot marker for every player (optional)

OBJECTIVES:
Score points for your team by getting your midaroni into the ring.

HISTORY:
We learned this activity from Mike Spiller, a good friend of ours, and an ultimate gamer. He tells us the game (the original with sticks) is played by the Eskimos of the far north. We're sure they will like this version.

PREPARATION:
Decide where to hang the ring-on-a-string, such as a tree branch, an overhead rafter, or a diving board (Oh, you'll need swim suits if you do this last one.).

You will want to hang the ring-on-a-string so that the ring is at the eye level of the players who will be standing or sitting (whichever you choose) in a circle around the ring - all those rings, are you dizzy yet?

SCENARIO:
It is the time of year when whales and walruses migrate close to your village. The animals are a necessary food for the village and they don't hang around to be a meal if your hunters miss. The hunters decide to form a game to choose the hunters with the best reflexes and focus to go out first.

INSTRUCTIONS:
Circle the players around the ring and number off by twos around the circle - the old 1,2,1,2,1,2,1,2,1,2 thing works well. Now give all the number ones a yellow noodle and the twos a purple noodle (whichever colors you have). Have each player extend his arm and noodle out (all the way) and touch the ring with the ends of the noodles. Place a spot marker down under one foot of each player. During the game players must have one foot on this spot at all times - of course the spot may not be moved. If the players are sitting, they must stay on their bottoms at all times.

Now, on to the game. Have the players touch their noodle to the ground. The leader will then spin the ring and call, "Start!" in a motivating voice. At this time the players can bring up their noodle and try to be the first player to put their noodle into the ring. Players may not sling the ring around or hold the ring out away from the group. If a player chooses to break any of the rules he or she is asked to step out of that round until a point is scored - joining in on the next round. Mike says, "This game is meant to be played with a 'Go For It' attitude - everyone going for the ring at the same time." Reset another round after each point is scored. The first team to 5 points wins the game. (We always like to play a best of five series.)

LEADER NOTES:
Keep one eye peeled for the over aggressive player(s). In the heat of the moment and all that stuff!

VARIATIONS:
Hang the ring-on-a-string off the end of a diving board. Have the teams suit up and tread water under the board to play this one. (A good leg workout!)

Noodle Jousting

GROUP SIZE:
Pairs

TIME:
10 - 15 minutes

PROPS:
- 2 Maxaronis
- 2 Minironis
- Masking tape

OBJECTIVES:
Knock the noodle off your opponent's shoulder and have fun.

HISTORY:
Sometimes you just gotta get goofy and have some fun. A customer wanted something quick to do in a limited space that would be fun and funny. In our initial tests we determined that balancing a minironi

on your shoulder was not good because it fell too easily and duct tape was too strong because even a severe noodle beating didn't knock the noodle off your shoulder. Sure, you might win the game, but it wasn't worth it.

PREPARATION:
Make a few rings of masking tape with the sticky side out. You will need these to stick a minironi on the shoulder of each of the players.

SCENARIO:
You and your nemesis, the Black Noodle Knight, have entered a jousting contest to determine the best Noodle Knight in the nation. Noodle Knights do not knock the knight from his horse but instead they need to nudge the noodle from near the neck of the opposing Noodle Knight.

INSTRUCTIONS:
Players each stick a minironi on their right shoulder. Each player gets a maxaroni and puts one end in their armpit while holding the rest of the noodle out like a jouster's lance. He then stands approximately 20 feet from his opponent.

The facilitator or one of the players says, "Are you ready?" and both players raise their lances straight up. Then, the speaker says, "Charge!" When the charge command is given, the players rush toward each other with maxaroni lances lowered under arm and attempt to knock the minironi from the shoulder of the other player. Players should never make contact with each other except with the Maxaronis.

An important note: The players should keep going past each other and not stop to knock off the minironi or make multiple swings. Letting the players stop and hit each other can be a safety hazard and it makes the game a matter of aggression rather than skill and focus (if you could qualify this as a skill and focus activity).

A player should come to a stop at the place where the other player started. If neither minironi has been knocked to the floor, the players should go for another pass using the same commands as before.

Players continue to joust until someone loses a minironi. In the event that both minironis are knocked off on the same pass, the player whose minironi touches the ground last wins.

LEADER NOTES:
This activity works best when played in pairs. More people will cause collisions. Several pairs can play independently at the same time as long as there is plenty of play space so people do not have to cross paths.

The full-length noodles (Maxaronis) make this game fun. The noodles are hard to aim because they wave up and down as people run or jog toward each other.

Many times the players do not realize when their minironi has been knocked off. Spectators can be helpful by watching and adding to the excitement by cheering.

VARIATIONS:
Add noodle horses for the players to ride. The horses can simply be midaronis or maxaronis or you can make your own version of noodle stick horses. There are also commercially-made noodle horses that squirt water.

? Problem-Solving ?

Problems or puzzles surround us each day. Where do I want to have lunch? Who can I ask to go with me to the mall? How much am I willing to spend for entertainment? What do I want to be when I grow up? All of these questions take skills to answer well. Even adults struggle with problems.

Problem-solving activities like the ones in this book have a variety of purposes. Like games, problem-solving activities can be fun and energizing; however, fun is not necessarily a key part of the solution process. After completing a tough problem, the feeling may be more like satisfaction, confidence, lesson learned, and self-esteem rather than fun. Problem-solving in a "no one is the expert" setting can teach us about who we are and how we handle ourselves around others.

Activities with a problem to solve tend to make people use more of their brain power than their physical strength. This characteristic enables a wide variety of people to participate and succeed.

As a leader, look more deeply into the lessons learned from solving problems with others, because challenges in life do not go away. Enjoy the problem solving activities and remain open to learning something about yourself and others as the facilitator or the participant.

Team O-pener

GROUP SIZE:
5 or more

TIME:
2 minutes

PROPS:
• 1 Midaroni for each person

OBJECTIVES:
Set the tone with a group showing that even though
they can work individually, the training they will

experience will be better if they work together.

HISTORY:
While using noodles as part of a "categories" activity, we noticed that the individuals who made their own circles struggled to keep their own noodles in a circle. The Team O-pener takes advantage of that dynamic to promote the idea of people working together instead of alone.

INSTRUCTIONS:
Everyone takes a midaroni and bends it into a circle so that the ends connect. What do you notice? (Typical observations include: It's hard to keep it together. You have to be strong.) Let these circles represent you today during the training.

Now, let's form one circle of noodles with the ends all connected. What do you notice this time? (Typical observations include: It's easier. I like that we are all together. It is bigger than we were individually.) Let this bigger circle represent where we are focusing today. Together the activities can be done more easily than working as individuals. In fact, one of the benefits to teamwork is that we can sometimes take a break to rejuvenate instead of working hard all the time. (The facilitator can let go of his noodle and it will stay suspended in the air in the circle.) Of course we will need to stay involved. Not everyone can step away or the circle will fall.

LEADER NOTES:
It is important to make your brief learning points and move on. I would suggest doing an activity like "Categories" or "Noodle Drop" following this quick demonstration.

Make sure when you let go of your noodle it will stay in place. Otherwise, the point may be lost.

VARIATIONS:
How few people can hold the noodles while maintaining the large circle?

Cubicles

Cubicles

GROUP SIZE:
10 to 20 people

TIME:
10-15 minutes

PROPS:
- 24 Midaronis
- 1 Stopwatch

OBJECTIVES:
Build a cube as quickly as possible using foam noodles.

HISTORY:
Cubicles is a fast-paced variation of a blindfold exercise from *50 Ways To Use Your Noodle* called 3-D Noodle Shapes. We needed a fast activity to illustrate the wisdom of teams to establish clear roles and responsibilities. It was amazing how quickly teams could build a cube from 12 then 24 foam noodles.

PREPARATION:
Count two sets of 12 midaronis and pile each set approximately 15 feet apart from each other.

SCENARIO:
In today's box manufacturing business time is money. We need to determine how fast a box can be made using the 12 noodles supplied to your team. When your team finishes a box, shout so I will know you are done. May the best team win.

(Do three rounds.)

In today's competitive marketplace it is sometimes best to combine your efforts to make something bigger. You have merged and now make 24-noodle boxes that are twice as big as before. Take a minute to strategize and then be ready to build while being timed.

(Do two or three rounds.)

INSTRUCTIONS:
Split the group in half and give 12 midaronis to each group.

Rules:
No one may touch the noodles before the start of each round. When you hear "Go!" build a cube out of your group's noodles as quickly as possible. Shout when you finish. Go!!

The two groups quickly construct their noodle shapes (hopefully without butting heads).

Try a couple or three rounds and see how quickly the groups can make the cubes.

Now, combine both groups and their resources and ask them to build a bigger cube using their 24 noodles. After a couple or three rounds, compare the times to the smaller cube times.

Often the larger cube takes less time to construct than the smaller ones.

LEADER NOTES:
In general, a team should be able to make one of the small cubes in 2 seconds and two teams with their combined resources can build one large cube in less than 2 seconds.

As with any energizing activity, it is helpful for the facilitator to keep things moving and be an energetic model for the teams.

I often move through the small cube building rounds quickly and then give a little time for the combined groups to organize themselves before starting the bigger cube building.

This is a good activity to use with two departments or companies that are merging.

VARIATIONS:
If you have enough people and noodles for three cubes, you can try to get one giant cube made at the end. The 36-noodle cube will be almost 8 feet tall.

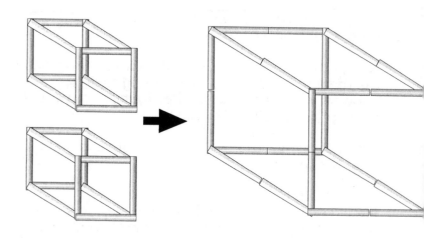

Noodle Cube

Noodle Cube

GROUP SIZE:
7 - 15 players

TIME:
30 minutes

PROPS:
• 12 Midaronis

OBJECTIVES:
Each team member passes through the cube without touching it.

HISTORY:
An activity that has been growing in popularity is the "Cube" made from PVC pipes and hung or balanced at a corner. The noodle cube takes advantage of this team problem solver and adds some more dynamics. The activity is similar to the spider's web except that the cube's holes tend to be larger, people do not have to be lifted, and everyone in the group stays involved.

SCENARIO:
Trapped in the computer, there is only one way out. A cube needs to be formed and each person needs to pass through the cube in a unique path without touching the frame. Any disruption of the framework (if the cube comes apart or the person passing through touches the frame) will create the need to restart.

INSTRUCTIONS:
The team gathers the 12 midaronis and forms a cube with all the pieces. When the team starts, this cube will need to stay together during the entire exercise. Your overall goal is for everyone in the group to pass through the cube without touching the noodles.

Each time a person passes through the cube, that path closes to the rest of the team. A cube has 30 unique paths if each path is considered one-way or 15 paths if you consider a path two-way.

Team members will hold the cube together. Available team members who do not have to hold the cube together will pass through the cube on their unique paths, then change roles with cube holders until everyone is through the cube.

If the cube ever becomes disconnected or the passer touches the cube frame, everyone will need to start the process over from the beginning. (You may want to have only the passer start over, depending on the level of challenge.)

LEADER NOTES:

The group should realize that the passer can avoid the cube frame or the frame can be moved to avoid the passer. The challenge for the group moving the cube is the coordination to keep the cube from falling apart. The cube often breaks apart early in the experience as people change roles from holders to passers.

I would suggest using different colored noodles so that the group can keep track of their paths more easily.

Letter Opener

GROUP SIZE:
10 to 30 plus players

TIME:
10 to 15 minutes

PROPS:
- At least 1 meatball for every player - If you play with fewer than 15 players, it's fun to have at least 2 meatballs per player.

OBJECTIVES:
Spell as many words as possible in the given amount of time.

HISTORY:
Our friend Steve Johnson got us started writing letters on the meatballs. We took this one right to a favorite of ours, "Scrabble Babble" found in, *Quicksilver* by Karl Rohnke -- shared with Karl by Garth Baker from New Zealand. Thanks everyone for the cool ideas!

PREPARATION:
You'll need some meatballs. If you don't have any cut yet, see the "Cutting Your Noodle" section at the beginning of this book. We prefer to use the Maxaroni Rex size, but they are sometimes hard to find. Using the Maxaroni/Midaroni size pieces works almost as well – they're just not as big.

For a standard set you will need 98 meatballs (this number coincides with the number of tiles in a standard Scrabble© set. When you have enough meatballs, print the letters you need on one side of the meatballs as big as you can with a permanent marker.

Okay, hope we don't get into any trouble for revealing any secret code. Here is what you need:
9-A, 2-B, 2-C, 4-D, 12-E, 2-F, 3-G, 2-H, 9-I, 1-J, 1-K, 4-L, 2-M, 6-N, 8-O, 2-P, 1-Q, 6-R, 4-S, 6-T, 4-U, 2-V, 2-W, 1-X, 2-Y, 1-Z.
We haven't used the number values at this point.

If you can get the Maxaroni Rex noodles, they will

probably have a hole in the center. Most letters will work around the hole – the bigger the letters the better. This standard set works well for groups of up to 30 players. If you work with more players, you know what to do. (NO, not quit! Cut some more noodles.)

SCENARIO:
(Use this idea if you want to process this process.) You are a data processing group hired to create as many words as you can in 5 minutes. What process can you develop to create the most words?

INSTRUCTIONS:
If you are working with a group of twelve or fewer, have each player get 1 meatball with a vowel on it and 1 with a consonant – each player will have 2 meatballs. If you have thirteen or more, have each player grab 1 meatball blindly out of the bag – or whatever you carry them around in. (This can be done before you give the instructions or after. Both ways will stimulate some interesting discussions.)

Tell the group to work together in some way to create as many different words as they can using the meatballs they have in their group – no trading from the bag once the game starts. You can leave the instructions at that or add a bit more. Once you make a word with a small group, you can move off to find different players to make another word – create words with different players each time. (We usually add this when working with big groups.)

LEADER NOTES:
The idea is to get players moving around and working with each other in a constructive way. The number of words created is not the main objective. We have observed many different methods of creating words, from staying together in one large group to breaking up into small groups and staying together, to everyone mingling around working with everyone they can. Utilize the activity in the best way to coincide with your objectives.

If it fits with our objectives and we have the time, we might go into Cross Words after Letter Opener.

VARIATIONS:
(Using the scenario above)
Provide pen and paper and really work together to create the longest list of words in 5 minutes.

NOTES:

_____

_____

_____

_____

_____

_____

_____

Cross Words

GROUP SIZE:
10 to 15 players

TIME:
10 to 15 minutes

PROPS:
- A standard set of lettered meatballs as described in Letter Opener.

OBJECTIVES:
Create a crossword-looking puzzle using all 98 lettered meatballs.

HISTORY:
We were looking for a filler one day and posed the challenge for a group to use all the meatballs in one giant crossword. It turned out to be a winner and a very interesting activity to watch as well.

PREPARATION:
If you haven't done so yet, you will need to create your lettered meatballs.

INSTRUCTIONS:
Create as many words as possible that follow the rules of a standard game of Scrabble© - only horizontal words from left to right and vertical words from top to bottom. Also, no words should be independent of any other words – all words should be connected. Pretend as if you were working on a large grid on the floor – all words must align with the other words in the rows and columns. Can the group use all 98 meatballs?

LEADER NOTES:
As we used this activity more and more there were some common behaviors. Some players got right down on the floor and started working. Others would help find letters that were being asked for. And some players just stood back and watched the action (often claiming that there was, "no room for them in the process") - lots of great things to talk about.

VARIATIONS:

If you are teaching math concepts, try using meatballs with numbers and math symbols like +, -, = and all those other ones I don't have on my keyboard. It is a pretty interesting challenge to use as many of the math meatballs as possible!

NOTES:

_____

_____

_____

_____

_____

_____

_____

Word Builder

Word Builder

GROUP SIZE:
10 to 30+ players

TIME:
10 to 15 minutes

PROPS:
- A standard set of lettered meatballs as described in Letter Opener
- Something to mark off a boundary area like cones, masking tape, or a string line. (You can find these lines, by the hundreds of feet, at your local hardware store. They work great for outlining boundaries and then you can roll them right back up on the spindle.)
- If you have some hula-hoops you can use one for each small group.

OBJECTIVE:
Small groups try to create 5-letter words as fast as possible.

HISTORY:
This activity is a close cousin to an activity that our friend Steve Johnson sent us. (We have included his suggestions below.) There are many different word-building games out there. With this one we added a little experiential twist. So, in the spirit of a great philosopher we know, "Anything worth doing, is worth overdoing!"

PREPARATION:
Create a large enough boundary area to set out all the meatballs, with the letters face down. You will want to place the meatballs far enough away from the boundary edges so players cannot reach in and grab any meatballs from the sides. Also, space out the meatballs enough for players to walk among them. As you will see, you want a large sized boundary area. Then if you have hula-hoops, place

them around the outside of the boundary area. Have one for every small group of three or four players – if you have 20 players you will want to set out 5 or 6 hula-hoops.

SCENARIO:

You have come together to brainstorm ideas for community building between areas of different cultures. As a group you first have to decide what words you will use to support your presentation on what a strong community needs – one different word for each small group. Then you must go through a process to complete these words that demonstrates true community. Upon completing this process you will take some time to evaluate what happened and determine if the words you chose were the words you used in your process. If you need to change any words, do so and then run the process again.

INSTRUCTIONS:

Split your large group up into smaller groups of three or four players. Have each group stand together outside of the boundary area. (If you have hula-hoops, have each group stand behind one.) Wherever the group is standing is their home base. This is where they will be building their word during the activity. (If they are using a hula-hoop have them make the word within the hoop.)

This is how to state it for full experiential effect: Each group will be making a five-letter word you would find in a standard American dictionary. The activity is not complete until everyone has a five-letter word spelled out at their home base area. Here are the additional parameters. Only one member from each small team can be in the letter area at one time. When a player enters the letter area they must grab a meatball, without looking at the letter, and bring it back to their home base before looking at it. Each group's home base can have no more than 5 letters at a time. If the team cannot use the letter that was brought back, the next player can take it back into the middle, place the meatball letter side down, and then grab another meatball from the area to bring back to the home base. This process continues until all the teams have a five-letter word.

If you choose to use the scenario above, you will also want to give the group some planning time to consider the words they want to use before they start spelling.

LEADER NOTES:
Here is the experiential twist. "The activity is not complete until everyone has a five-letter word..." What we often observe is small teams working really hard to complete their word. When they are done, they think "they" are done. Our questions to them would be, "Are you done?" "Are you sure?" "What is the objective?" And if we have to go there, "What can you do, within the guidelines, to reach the objective?"

One of the solutions might be the players going in to get a meatball. Going back to their home base looking at the letter, then bringing the letter out to the middle and shouting out what letter it is. Another solution we have seen is the players asking the other teams, who are still working, what they need and then going off to find it. We have yet to see the small teams initially working in this way to achieve the objective. So far we have had to "guide" them into that direction.

VARIATIONS:
Here are a few of Steve's ideas. Have all the meatballs in a box in the middle of the boundary area. Then pose any one of these challenges following the same process guidelines above: 1) Form as many words as possible in two minutes. (You can have more than 5 meatballs at your home base), 2) Score the highest possible points within one minute. (You will need to add the point values to the meatballs), or, 3) The first team to spell the names of all their team members. Here's one we added, how

about each team doing a Cross Words (see Cross Words) at their home base.

NOTES:

_____

_____

_____

_____

_____

_____

Squares

GROUP SIZE:
2 - 10 people for each puzzle

TIME:
10 - 30 minutes

PROPS:
• 12 Midaronis

PREPARATION:
What we like to do is ask each individual to solve the puzzle on his or her own without touching the noodles. They can work on paper if needed. This allows each player to have the chance to solve the puzzle before the answer is given. After a reasonable amount of time to solve the puzzle, ask one of the players to move the noodles into the answer. You might be surprised to discover more than one answer to the puzzles.

INSTRUCTIONS:
Using the 12 midaronis set up as shown, try the following puzzles. The noodles do not need to be bent or cut in any way to solve the puzzles.

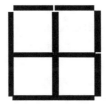

A) Remove 2 noodles, leaving 2 squares of different sizes.

B) Move 3 noodles to form 3 identical squares.

C) Move 4 noodles to form 3 identical squares.

D) Move 2 noodles to form 7 squares. [Not all the squares are identical. You are allowed to cross noodles over each other.]

E) Move 4 noodles to form 10 squares. [Not all the squares are identical. You are allowed to cross noodles over each other.]

LEADER NOTES:
The information in the brackets is optional. They can be hints if the players ask for them.

VARIATIONS:

F) Save the Pig from the arrow by moving only 2
   noodles. (If the players choose to move the
   arrow's head, congratulate them and ask them to
   try again, this time without moving the noodles of
   the arrow.) The solution requires a healthy
   imagination.

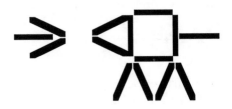

(Solutions are found on page 184)

Meatball Puzzles

Meatball Puzzles

GROUP SIZE:
2 to 12 players or more if you have lots of meatballs

TIME:
10 to 20 minutes

PROPS:
- Several meatballs depending on the puzzle and number of players (but no more than the 98 in your standard set of meatballs as described in Letter Opener).

OBJECTIVES:
Players work together on lateral thinking skills to solve puzzles.

HISTORY:
The stick games were so much fun; we thought we would add these to or bag of tricks. Coin games have been around since the coin itself. So, like other games in this book, why not make-um macro.

PREPARATION:
All you need is a bunch of meatballs ready for whatever puzzle you present.

INSTRUCTIONS:
Present one of the following puzzles and then let small groups go off with the meatballs they need to work out the answer.

A) **The Cross Challenge**

Take 6 meatballs and place them out in the shape of a cross, like this,

```
        O
    O   O   O
        O
        O
```

Now move just one of the meatballs and create two rows of four meatballs in each.

B) **Pyramid of Meatballs**

Lay 10 meatballs out like this,

```
        O
      O   O
    O   O   O
  O   O   O   O
```

Now move just three of the meatballs and turn the pyramid upside down.

C) **Rows**

Take seven meatballs and arrange them in a pattern to look like the letter H.

```
    O       O

    O   O   O

    O       O
```

This H pattern contains 5 rows. 3 meatballs in each row. Add just 2 more meatballs to make 10 rows with 3 meatballs in each row.

D) Odd Lines
Take 12 meatballs and lay them out in a very familiar pattern, so that you end up with three straight lines and an odd number of meatballs in each line.

E) Seven Rows
Take 12 meatballs and lay them out in seven rows, with four meatballs in each row.

LEADER NOTES:
There are just a few here of the multitude of coin games out there. We bet you can peruse your local library or bookstore for more choice puzzles.

(Solutions are found on page 185)

Oh the Pressure

Oh the Pressure

GROUP SIZE:
10 to 15 players

TIME:
15 to 20 minutes

PROPS:
- 1 Midaroni for each player
- An index card for each player

OBJECTIVES:
Pass the midaronis around to create a circle without dropping the index cards pressed between each end of the midaronis.

HISTORY:
Rex Wadsworth of Mansfield, Texas passed on this activity to us. He added this challenge to one of his groups while they were all standing on top of a telephone pole (It was lying on its side on the ground at the time.). We added the index cards to the mix for a little excitement.

PREPARATION:
You will want to prepare the index card challenges before you start this one – if you want to attempt this variation. We've listed some challenges below in the variation section.

SCENARIO:
You have been dispatched to assemble a communication dish in the jungles of South America to relay an important message destined to enhance World Peace. You have brought along with you all the components necessary to assemble the dish. To receive the message with the dish, it must be turning counterclockwise for 30 seconds without any break in the dish components. Every additional 10 seconds will relay the message again. We know that people are more likely to retain information if they hear it

more than once. Once you have relayed the message, disassemble the dish, carefully, and move to another area to relay the message.

INSTRUCTIONS:
Ask the group to make a circle facing in towards the center. Have all the midaronis and index cards near one part of the circle. Follow these assembly instructions for disk assembly and operation:

One component is added to the process at a time in the following order, noodle, index card, noodle, index card, and so on until all the components are in the dish – the cards are pressed between the noodles.

The components are added into the process at the same point in the circle.

All the components are passed/pressed around the circle as additional components are added.

If any component is dropped, the process must stop until the dropped components(s) are placed back into the assembly.

When all the components are added, the ends are joined together, closing the circle, with an index card pressed between them.

Once assembled the dish must move in a counterclockwise direction for at least 30 seconds to pick up and send the message. Continue, if possible, up to 60 seconds to ensure extended communication.

If any component is dropped in the process, it must be added back to the dish. Since the signal will be lost whenever there is a break, the time starts again.

LEADER NOTES:
The idea here is for the group to create a rotating circle with the noodles while pressing index cards between each end of each noodle. This activity takes quite a bit of communication and patience. And it's

very interesting to watch.

VARIATIONS:
The original description called for the group to make a line and then pass and press the noodles together down the line without any noodles separating. And, this was done while standing on a telephone pole (that was on the ground).

You can add a little fun to the process by putting some challenges on the index cards. If an index card drops to the ground during the process – either in a circle or a line – the group has to perform the challenge while continuing to pass and press the noodles. Here are a few card challenges we have used: Every other player must stand on one foot for 20 seconds. The two players closest to where the card dropped must close their eyes for 30 seconds. The group has to sing two rounds of row-row-row your boat. The two players closest to the card when it lands can only use one hand for the next 15 seconds. The group can only talk while their lips are over their teeth for the next 30 seconds.

Read each card aloud before it is added to the process to prepare the group for the possible consequence. It's interesting to listen to the group as the cards go around, "Here comes the lip one! Be careful."

What Can You Make of It

What Can You Make of It

GROUP SIZE:
10 to 20 players

TIME:
10 to 15 minutes

PROPS:
• 1 Midaroni for each player

OBJECTIVES:
Work with a partner to create different objects using the noodles.

HISTORY:
This activity was picked up, by accident actually, by Chris during a training session at Honey Rock Camp up in northern Wisconsin. A small group of participants were using their time, waiting for the other group to arrive from their noodle walk. We love those sorts of accidents.

SCENARIO:
You are a creative development team working on new product lines for developed resources. Brainstorm as many product possibilities in 5 minutes.

INSTRUCTIONS:
Pair up players (A group of three will work as well.). Make sure each player has 1 midaroni. Give about a 1-minute planning window before you start. The idea is for each pair to use their 2 noodles to create some sort of object – using the noodles. For example, putting the two noodles together in two arch forms and calling it, "The Golden Arches." Or, circle one noodle around a person's head and arching the other over the top and calling it, "A hat." So, when you start, the idea is to continue around the circle of pairs. As soon as one pair shares their idea, the next pair should be ready to share their idea and so on.

Keeping the ideas flowing is the concept. If a pair isn't ready they can call, "pass." We find that 3 times around seems to get the juices going. Then go into a fun game of "Noodle Speed Rabbit."

LEADER NOTES:
This turns out to be a fun energizer and great for a small team communication/problem solving challenge. Getting pairs to work together is one of the first steps to getting larger groups to work together.

VARIATIONS:
You could give the groups a theme like, household appliances or recreation equipment. You could also have the other groups try to guess what the pair is demonstrating before the next pair goes. How about a game of "Noodlary?" (Pictionary with noodles)

Team Up, Over, & In

GROUP SIZE:
10 to 30 players

TIME:
15 to 25 minutes

PROPS:
• As many meatballs as you have available (A
  standard set of 98 as described in Letter Opener is
  a good number. You won't need the letters for
  this one however).

- A container that can hold all the meatballs at one time. (Sam's favorite is a pop-up laundry basket found at any of those larger department stores that start with a W or a T (No free ads!).
- 4 Items you can stick at the corners of the boundary area, like cones, coats, or frozen chickens.

OBJECTIVES:
Return all the meatballs to the container as fast as possible.

HISTORY:
We picked this one up from our friend Mike Spiller, L.T.D.F. (Licensed to Deliver Fun).

PREPARATION:
Place a container in the center of a 40' x 40' boundary area (or whatever size you want to work with). Then, evenly disperse the meatballs around within the boundaries.

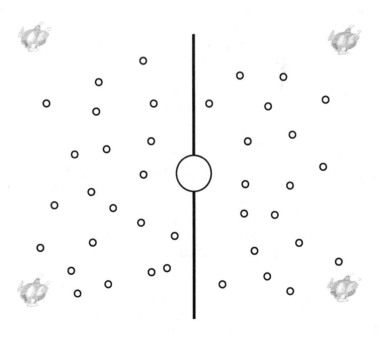

SCENARIO:
Being part of a successful basketball team means practice and lots of it. Today the whole team is working on its passing and alley-oop techniques. All the noodles on the floor represent balls that need to be put into the basket. No one can make a basket directly. The only baskets that count are the ones that have been passed to the final shooter. This is a timed activity. The faster we can get all the noodles into the basket, the better.

INSTRUCTIONS:
Gather your group around the boundaries for the instructions.

As a team you will be working together to replace all the meatballs back into the container. Point out that there are two sides within the boundary, the North (to the North of the container) and the South (to the... you know). (If you are working in certain parts of the country, you might use East and West?) Split your group in half and send each to one side of the boundary area.

This is how it plays out. On the signal to begin, all the players can go to a meatball, pick it up and toss it to the other side. The player must toss the meatball from where he finds it. The object is to throw the meatball so that a player on the other side can catch it. A meatball caught can be placed into the container. (Meatballs that fly into the container "on accident" should be removed from the container and placed back out into the boundary area. Sometimes we even add a penalty that another two have to come out as well.) If a meatball happens to touch the ground again after it is caught, it must be thrown back to someone on the other side to be caught and then containered.

This entire process is timed until the last meatball is caught and then placed into the container. Then, you can challenge the group to better their time. With a little planning and problem solving, anything is possible!

LEADER NOTES:
This is a great one to play after Mars Attacks (*50 Ways to Use Your Noodle*) to get all the meatballs picked up. Actually it is a great activity to do anytime you need meatballs or minironis gathered.

NOTES:

_____

_____

_____

_____

_____

_____

_____

Javel-in Throw

GROUP SIZE:
8 to 16 players

TIME:
20 to 25 minutes

PROPS:
- 2 Midaronis for every small team of three to four players
- 3 Spots or cones for every small team
- 1 Large container like a garbage can or big box – the size of the container will determine the challenge you want to give the group. The larger the container, the easier the activity seems to be.

OBJECTIVES:
Throw the noodles into a large target to gain as many points as possible in a given amount of time.

HISTORY:
Our friend Kip Prichard shared this idea with us. It has been a great hit with our younger groups and seems to bring out the youth in the older groups.

PREPARATION:
Place the large container in the middle of the playing area you plan to use. You will need to set out a line of spots (or cones) for every small team you have playing. Let's say you have a group of twelve players. If you split them into four groups of three players, you'll need 4 lines. For each line the firsts spot will be 5 feet from the container, the second spot will be 10 feet from the container, and the third spot is 15 feet from the container. All 3 spots are in a row and in a line towards the container looking like the spokes on a wheel. You're ready.

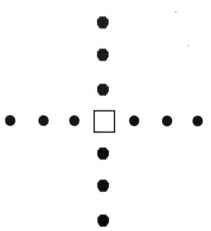

SCENARIO:
B.Y.O.A. has been a superior arrow manufacturing plant for the past fifty years. They are especially famous for their handmade specialty arrows used to relocate kiwis to the grasslands of New Zealand.

(The arrows stun, but do not injure the birds.) One reason for the company's success is the speed that they can pack the arrows for shipment. You are part of the packing team ready for the latest workout in their new training/observation room. Work fast, aim well, and have fun; it will ensure the company's success and your employment.

INSTRUCTIONS:
Whatever size group you have you will want to divide them up into groups of three or four players. Then, each small team will need a line of spots as described above. When divided, ask each team to stand behind one of the furthest spots away from the container – each team having their own line. Hand out 2 midaronis to each team – if you can give each small team a different color it might help the process, but it isn't necessary.

Here's the challenge to the group as a whole. They have 1 minute to make as many points as possible. The closest spot to the container is worth 1 point, the middle spot is 3 points, and the farthest spot is worth 5 points. To make any points a player must stand on a spot of choice and throw the Javel in the container (That would be the noodle – but you knew that!). The Javel must remain in the container for the points to count. Players get one throw per turn and them must go to the end of their team line. Use the second noodle to assist the team's speed – one player throwing, another on deck with a noodle, then rotating from there. Ask each small team to keep track of its own score. Then add the small team score together to get the group total.

Provide about one minute for planning before each round. Decisions have to be made about which spot to throw from. Who will be getting the noodle after it is thrown? What about that container; is it going to stay upright? Who will be responsible for keeping the score? Remember, this is a large group team effort – working together separately to achieve a common goal. We usually allow three rounds with planning between each round – giving them the opportunity to discuss changes that will improve their overall score as group.

LEADER NOTES:

Often times we will explain the activity and let them start right away without any planning time before the first round. We provide the experience first and then let them plan based on the setbacks from there. Without the experience they can only speculate on what might happen. Besides, when we do this the score is usually low so it is easier to beat after they do a little problem solving.

VARIATIONS:

You could use meatballs to do this one as well. A take on the activity "Pick and Choose" from *Silver Bullets* by Karl Rohnke.

Team Write

GROUP SIZE:
4 - 8 writers

TIME:
15 - 30 minutes

PROPS:
- 1 Minironi or midaroni with a hole through the middle
- 1 Colored marker - Water-based markers wash off of the floor and people better than permanent markers do.
- Approximately 5 feet of string or cord for each participant.
- A surface to write on such as flip cart paper

OBJECTIVES:
A team writes or draws by all using the same marker.

HISTORY:
In a workshop many years ago, I saw a demonstration activity to illustrate one of the challenges of teamwork. A group of four people held the same pencil and attempted to write one of the team member's names on a sheet of paper. They could not start until they had the same name in mind. Was it going to be printed or cursive? They did finally finish the task after printing the shortest name in the group. This noodle activity works well with kids and adults.

PREPARATION:
Tie string around the noodle so that when the players pull the ends, the device will look like spokes on a wheel with the noodle at the hub. Each player should have an end to hold. Each string need not be more than 5 feet long. Even 2-foot strings work well.

Push a marker into the hole of the noodle leaving an inch or two sticking out. (Keep the cap on the marker until the team is ready to go, otherwise it's a mess.)

Lay the paper on the floor (You might want to tape it down.) and decide what you want the team to draw or write.

SCENARIO:

You are all part of a global company with locations throughout the world. Each of you is used to pulling your own weight to make the company successful; however, a new customer wants to see how well your people work together. Do they share the same vision? Can they really work together to create what the customer needs - on time and to their quality standards?

Your first task is to draw your company logo within the next five minutes using your network communication system.

INSTRUCTIONS:

Everyone take hold of the end of a string on your team's writing device. Organize yourselves so that the strings are not crossed or tangled.

I will be calling out something for you to draw with the marker stuck in the noodle. Draw the item and then I will call out something else. Please hold the strings at the ends only and do not touch the marker or its holder. This activity is not about finding loopholes or tricks; it is about working together.

LEADER NOTES:

Straight lines tend to be easier than curves. Placing the marker at specific locations on the drawing is a challenge.

A progression of pictures might include the following: Square, circle, smiley face, someone's name, a house, a picture of the president.

To add to the challenge, use a midaroni and tie the strings at different levels along the noodle.

VARIATIONS:

Solve a maze that has been enlarged. Mike Spiller takes his mazes to a print shop to have them enlarged and laminated. He uses a dry erase marker so that the same maze can be used again and again.

Tape the writing surface to the wall.

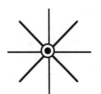

~ Water Ways ~

In the first *50 Ways To Use Your Noodle* book, we included activities that were only intended to experience on dry land or indoors on the floor. The noodles are made and sold to use in the water; however, many places can only use water activities for a short season. The first noodle book was partly written to answer the question, "What can we do with all these noodles in the winter?" This new book continues that theme and adds several pool/water activities that are fun and unusual.

A few things you may want to know about noodles and water include spitting, cleaning, and drying. Spitting noodles refers to propelling a meatball by pinching it on the edge. A meatball can travel 20 feet or more if you pinch it and let it pop out of your fingers. It reminds me of squirting watermelon seeds. This dynamic only works when the meatball is wet.

Many people have asked about cleaning the noodles after groups have used them for land activities. One benefit to the water games is that the water and chlorine clean the noodles. The game, Submersion, is a great way to quickly clean everything you have.

Once you have used the noodles in the water, you may need to dry them quickly for a land activity. The longer the noodles have been wet, the more water they have likely soaked up. The noodle's air bubbles that have been burst act like small water containers. Hitting the noodles or swinging them around quickly will eliminate some of the excess water. As we mentioned at the beginning of the book, the microwave or fireplace is not a good option to dry your noodles. Put the noodles in a mesh bag and hang it in a breezy area or consider tying the bag to your vehicle and taking a drive. If you are desperate, a clothes dryer set to "no heat" drying will work for minironis and meatballs. How do we know all these things? It's better you didn't know.

Submersion

GROUP SIZE:
2 - 10 players at a time

TIME:
10 - 30 minutes

PROPS:
• Approximately 100 or more noodles of any shape

and size

OBJECTIVES:
Completely submerge all the noodles in the pool as a team.

PREPARATION:
Put all the noodles in the pool. Don't worry about keeping them together.

SCENARIO:
Oh no! Someone has dumped the Frog Ovum Activation Media (FOAM) into the pool! If we don't deactivate the eggs, we'll be up to our armpits in frogs within the hour.

This scientific research project was designed to grow frogs at an extremely high rate of speed by simply dropping FOAM in South American and African waterways. The intent was to manage mosquitos and malaria. Now all the FOAM has been activated in this one pool! There is only one way to stop the process. Hold all the FOAM completely underwater for ten seconds.

INSTRUCTIONS:
All the noodles in the pool need to be completely submerged at the same time for 10 seconds. No props such as bags, nets, towels, or clothing may be used to keep the noodles under the water. It is just you against the noodles.

To start the game, all of the available noodles need to be floating and no one may be touching them. The facilitator says, "GO" to start the challenge. When all the noodles are submerged, someone in the team needs to shout, "Noodles Down!" The facilitator and team will then count to ten. If a noodle (or a part of a noodle) comes up out of the water during the count, a "Submersion" hasn't happened and the team can try again.

When the team successfully keeps the noodles down

for the count of ten an official Submersion has occurred.

LEADER NOTES:
Meatballs and minironis challenge the team because they are difficult to gather and keep under the water at the same time without them popping up. Midaronis or Maxaronis are especially challenging because they float so well that lightweight players may have difficulty pushing them under.

This is definitely not one of those activities where one person does all the work while everyone else watches.

VARIATIONS:
It is hard to keep a good noodle down, but to add more challenge to this activity just add more noodles or challenge the team to a timed event. We are looking for the world's fastest Submersion timed from "Go" to "Noodles Down!"

Noodle Tight Rope

GROUP SIZE:
4-10

TIME:
15-45 minutes

PROPS:
• 4-5 Midaronis or 3-4 Maxaronis

OBJECTIVES:
Walk from one edge of the pool to the other without touching the bottom of the pool.

HISTORY:
This activity originated from an experiment to see if a person could stay afloat while walking on a midaroni in the deep end of the pool. It worked, but not very well. It was more like just balancing on the noodle. We discovered that combining balance on a noodle at the bottom of the pool with more people could get you places.

PREPARATION:
Select a path you want the group to travel. If you want, you can even mark a path with coins, rings, or washers. Be sure not to make the group get more than chest deep or they will have a hard time staying

on the bottom. Shallow water is the most challenging. Please be cautious to keep the group from falling and hitting the edge of the pool.

SCENARIO:
After your ship sank, you thought you might never make it. The experience is not over yet. You and your group have floated to a coral reef surrounding a beautiful island. You would just walk to the beach, but the corals are very sharp and will cut your feet. Fortunately, you have some floatation aids that have kept you afloat until now and may be used to protect your feet. Unfortunately, you realize that hungry ethafoam flounders have surrounded you. This species of flounder is a very aggressive top water feeder. They especially like foam noodles with a side of human. Your only hope is to keep the noodles under the water, walk slowly, and not bleed as you make your way to the safety of dry land.

INSTRUCTIONS:
Starting at the edge of the pool, travel along the marked path to the other side. Because the pool floor is hazardous to human contact, use the noodles as a protective barrier to walk on.
Rules:
- Once a noodle has been placed underwater it cannot come out of the water.
- Human contact with the bottom of the pool or the edge of the pool along your journey can be hazardous.
- Treading water and swimming are strictly forbidden. (At least one foot must be touching a noodle.)
- Your journey is complete when the last person in the group touches the finish

LEADER NOTES:
This can be a very challenging activity for teams. Typically, a noodle coming out or the water causes a restart. Touching the bottom or sides of the pool, swimming, or treading water can cause a variety of challenges such as an unstoppable urge to hold the

back of your neck or goggle eyes (swim goggles with duct tape covering or partially covering the lenses).

Monitoring touches to the bottom of the pool can be difficult. This is a great opportunity for the group to exercise integrity. When people lose their balance, it is usually not difficult to see swimming and treading happen.

VARIATIONS:
You can use meatballs as a substitute for the midaronis; just offer the same number of meatballs as people plus one or two.

NOTES:

_____

_____

_____

_____

_____

_____

_____

Raft Building

GROUP SIZE:
5-15 people

TIME:
30-60 minutes

PROPS:
- 80 - 100 Maxaronis or more midaronis
- String, thin rope, or webbing. Thin string tends to be hard on the noodles because it cuts the foam easily.
- White cloth and paint or permanent marker for a flag (optional)

OBJECTIVES:
Build a raft to support your whole team.

HISTORY:
People have used raft construction for team building for many years. The foam noodles are especially good materials because they have no sharp edges, are lightweight, and float very well.

PREPARATION:
Locate a safe place to launch the raft. It is wise to have life jackets.

INSTRUCTIONS:
Build a raft that will support the entire team. You may use any of the materials provided.

LEADER NOTES:
To build the raft (one common way) the noodles are arranged in groups of 10 or 12 and lashed side by side (like a flat bamboo mat). This makes a small quarter raft about 3' X 6' in size. Four of these are then lashed together to make one big one, and then another four quarters are put on top (going in the opposite direction) to make a pretty bombproof raft for 15 people! This uses about 80-100 noodles that weigh very little and take up about as much space as four or five 55-gallon drums. You don't need planks, but you use a bunch of string or rope. The whole thing is a lot softer, has no splinters, much lower density than wood and metal, and doesn't flip over as easily as some barrel and plank designs.

VARIATIONS:
Add a fishing task to a subgroup who's job it is to use the fishing line and hook they are given to (I bet you could guess.) catch a fish or two from off the completed raft.

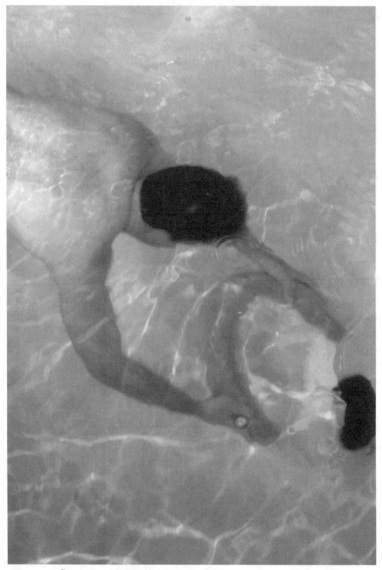

Sunken Treasure

GROUP SIZE:
2-10 players

TIME:
10 - 30 minutes

PROPS:
- 2-4 Midaronis
- Various items that will sink to the bottom of the pool such as rings, diver weights, chair, etc. (Even a bowling ball will work.)

OBJECTIVES:
Retrieve one or more objects from the bottom of the pool using midaronis.

PREPARATION:
Toss sinkable objects into the pool in or near the deep end.

SCENARIO:
You have discovered some amazing treasures at the bottom of the ocean and want to dive down to retrieve them. Unfortunately, the treasures lay on a volcano that has heated the treasures beyond human tolerance. You have some special tools that can stand the heat. Using these tools, get all the treasures you can.

INSTRUCTIONS:
Swim under the water to retrieve the objects on the bottom of the pool. The only things that can touch the objects until they reach the surface are the noodles.

LEADER NOTES:
Many people use a midaroni like tweezers to pick up various objects from the bottom of the pool. The task quickly turns from, "How are we going to use the noodle to get the object?" to "How can we get the noodle down to the bottom?" Teamwork will work.

Depending on the object, a solution for some objects may be to slip a noodle under them or in a hole in the object and let the noodle do all the lifting. This technique doesn't work for the bowling ball.

VARIATIONS:
Simply have people touch a midaroni to the bottom
of the pool. Go for two... three!

NOTES:

_____

_____

_____

_____

_____

_____

_____

Reverse Stacking

GROUP SIZE:
2-10

TIME:
10 - 30 minutes

PROPS:
• 18-25 Meatballs per stacker is ideal

OBJECTIVES:
Create a stack of noodles under the water.

INSTRUCTIONS:
<u>Version 1</u> -
While you are in the water put your hand on the water and place a meatball under your hand. Now put another meatball under the first. Once a meatball has been placed, it cannot be repositioned later. Continue this reverse stacking until the stack explodes to the surface. Your holding hand can stay on the water's surface or it can go under the water. Feel free to work with a partner or two and have them place the meatballs on the bottom of the stack one at a time.

<u>Version 2</u> -
While you are in the water put a meatball on the water, place your hand on it, and push it down into the water until your hand touches the water. You can lift your hand out of the water and place another meatball under the first, then push the two noodles until your hand touches the water. When you push the noodles beneath the water and touch your hand into the water it is called a "Tag Out." Each time you add a new meatball you can raise your hand and the stack of noodles with it; however, you have to tag out before placing the next noodle.

LEADER NOTES:
Version 1 is more difficult because the noodles become more unstable and harder to hold down as you stack. Version 2 is much more dynamic because you can get taller stacks that require a lot of "reverse balancing" to keep them from falling apart. When the stacks get beyond 15 meatballs, they start acting like a leash connected to a small-excited dog. You will have to try it to know what I mean.

8 Seconds

GROUP SIZE:
This is a solo activity. Small groups can take turns with one mesh horse.

TIME:
Well, if you want to be literal – 8 seconds (or less). However, I'm sure you could spend 15 to 20 minutes on this one.

PROPS:
• At least 15 to 24 midaronis inside of a mesh laundry bag

• A body of water.

OBJECTIVES:
Stay on top of the mesh bull for 8 seconds.

HISTORY:
When our mesh bag of midaronis fell into the pool, the light bulb went off and the rest IS history. The time of 8 seconds refers to the time a rodeo bull rider needs to stay on the bull.

PREPARATION:
You will want to prepare your mesh bull (the mesh bag of noodles) for the weight of your players. The more noodles in the bag will keep the bull out of the water more than fewer noodles. Lighter players will have the greatest challenge with many noodles in the bag. You can adjust when needed.

SCENARIO:
You have all made it to the World Water Rodeo championships. This event is the bucking mesh noodle bull. Try to stay on the bull, above the water, for 8 seconds.

INSTRUCTIONS:
The idea here is to stay atop the mesh bag of noodles while sitting on it the way you would sit on a horse western style – straddled. There are a couple of ways to mount the bull. Get into the water with the mesh noodle bull. Stay clear of any object that you could bump into. Then try to mount the bull getting one leg over. At first you could have someone hold the bag while mounting. For an added challenge, try to get on without anyone holding. The second mount is fun but a bit more dangerous. This mount is done by jumping onto the mesh bull from the side of the pool or pier. The obvious concern is head-to-hard-surface danger. Make sure the mesh noodle bull is well away from the edge of any danger when attempting this mount. If a player is able to balance quite well for a long time, try a few Cannonballs in his general direction – ALWAYS keeping safety at the front of

mind! (This means, don't cannonball on top of the rider!)

LEADER NOTES:
Safety, Safety, Safety!!

VARIATIONS:
For less or more challenge, here are a few adjustments. These will cause different reactions in different players. Hook or unhook the feet under the bull. Don't touch the bag with your hands. Grab hold of the bag with one hand and swing the free arm up and down like a real cowboy – this gets that bull going up and down in the water for an added ride and challenge.

Chicken Noodle

GROUP SIZE:
4 to 10 players

TIME:
5 to 15 minutes for several games

PROPS:
• 1 to 4 Midaronis per player depending on the
  weight of each player

OBJECTIVES:
Be the last chicken noodle in the water.

HISTORY:
Most of us remember Chicken Fighting in the water. Here's a bit safer way to play.

INSTRUCTIONS:
Have the players get into the water and place some midaronis behind their knees (not between their knees) – enough to hold each player up when she leans back into the water. There should be enough noodles to pull the player's legs out of the water when leaning back (You may need to be flexible with this rule.). A legal chicken noodle must have at least one of her noodles up out of the water (at least a majority of it). In this position, the players will need to use their arms in a treading motion to keep their heads out of the water – breathing is better done above water. (This treading ability will be necessary to play this game.)

After a bit of practice moving around and staying up in this position, players go out away from any solid objects (like the side of the pool) and try to dislodge the other chicken noodle players. Players may not touch any other player's noodles during dislodging. And, pulling hair is not a nice thing! However, a well-aimed splash or shove on the shoulder works well. A dislodged player will be one that is flipped over, thus losing the noodles from behind her knees.

It is possible for a player to be flipped over and still have their noodles under their knees. If they can come back up and have their noodles showing above the water, they can continue play.

LEADER NOTES:
This game can get frantic. It will be VERY important to monitor safe play during the activity. Make sure all players understand the nature of this game before getting involved. And, as a safety measure, make sure you have a way to stop play quickly, like blowing a whistle.

VARIATIONS:
This can also be a team-against-team activity if everyone wants to play in this scenario.

NOTES:

_____

_____

_____

_____

_____

_____

Snow Cone

Snow Cone

GROUP SIZE:
3 to 6 players per beach ball

TIME:
10 to 15 minutes

PROPS:
- 1 Midaroni for each player
- A good size beach ball for each group of 3 to 6 players. Have additional beach balls available for multiple trips.

OBJECTIVES:
Move a beach ball across the pool atop the noodle ends.

HISTORY:
We have seen some great team development using the activity Funky Dunk found in the first 50 Ways to Noodle. So, we moved this one to the water. It doesn't require as many noodles since the ball is much lighter.

SCENARIO:
You are a group of anthropologists studying the nesting patterns of the great Teilamoda. Today, after studying a certain nest for the last 3 months, you noticed that all the eggs were moved out into the open – you assume by another animal that most likely has the intention of using these eggs for sustenance. To save the study at hand you decide to move the eggs back to the original nest before the mother returns. You have all the appropriate equipment but find one obstacle in the way...

INSTRUCTIONS:
Using only the midaroni noodle ends, move the beach ball(s) through the pool from the shallow across to the deep end and back to shore on the other side of the pool. (If you have a lake scenario,

try to work out a shallow to deeper path.) The beach ball(s) can only touch the noodles during the crossing. Each player can only touch one noodle during the activity. If a beach ball falls into the water, or touches the water, it must be returned to the starting side before going across again.

LEADER NOTES:
If your group travels from a shallow spot to a deeper spot, that will require treading water, make sure all the players going into the deep end will be able to tread.

VARIATIONS:
For an easier progression, just use a shallow crossing so everyone can touch the bottom. Or, use half the group (some non-treaders) to travel the shallow end, then have them transfer the beach ball to another group who will take it through the deep end.

Noodle Hug

GROUP SIZE:
1 player (This is a one player challenge, however, other players can take turns as they challenge each other.)

TIME:
As long as interest is available

PROPS:
• 10 to 15 Midaronis

OBJECTIVES:
Jump into the water with as many noodles as you can without letting any fly out of your arms.

HISTORY:
One day we said, "This would be interesting, let's give it a go." (Really, we said <u>that</u>, "Give it a go!")

INSTRUCTIONS:
The idea here is to grab as many midaroni noodles in your arms – giving them a big hug. Then jump off the edge of the pool AWAY FROM THE EDGE and into the deep end, or deep enough water. Can you come up with all the noodles you left with? If you can, add another noodle, if not, try again or take away one of the noodles. What will be your maximum noodle hug count?

LEADER NOTES:
AWAY FROM THE EDGE is a very important factor here! You might want keep a watchful eye and a pair of hands ready for some spotting. Running and jumping is not a good option.

VARIATIONS:
Let the players add a leg wrap around the noodles before hitting the water.

Use meatballs or minironis.

Swim-N-Spell

GROUP SIZE:
8 to 20 players

TIME:
15 to 25 minutes

PROPS:
• A standard set of lettered meatballs (98) as described in Letter Opener

• A pool setting is best. However, if you have a roped swimming area and still water, it should work fine.

OBJECTIVES:
Be the first team to acquire all the letters to spell a five-letter word.

HISTORY:
We have so much fun with Word Builder we decided to bring this one to the water.

PREPARATION:
Place your lettered meatballs face down at one end of the pool or swim area.

SCENARIO:
Your ship is sinking and you and your crewmates need to send a simple message consisting of one word with five letters to the approaching helicopter. Because of the danger, only one of your crew can gather a letter at a time. If the message is incomplete or too slowly formed, the helicopter may leave the area without providing a rescue.

INSTRUCTIONS:
Depending on the size of your body of water, split your group up into even size teams – we would suggest at least three on a team to provide adequate rest between turns.

Tell the group that their objective will be to form a five-letter word. This will be done by one person from each team going out into the water at a time, swimming to the letters and bringing one back. This process continues until the word is formed.

Groups cannot determine what word they will make until the first player comes back with a letter. This first letter must appear in the final five-letter word. So, after the first letter is back to the group, they all decide what five-letter word they want to make. Then the next player can go out into the water for another letter. Letters do not have to come back in a particular order. Meatballs may not be thrown back to the team; they must be swum back and handed to the team. Only one letter can be brought back at a time, and, unlike Word Builder, the players can look for the letter they need before they take a meatball back. Letters will be flopping up during the activity, why fight it?

The first team to create their word wins the round or game, how ever you are playing it.

LEADER NOTES:
There will be some treading involved if the letters are placed out into deeper water. Make sure all players will be able to do so. And, this goes without saying, but our little voices… watch the letter area closely – lots a thrashing in this area!

VARIATIONS:
You can start with a four-letter word, then go a five, then maybe one more round to a six-letter word.

You can play the five-letter word. Then the winner of each round must go to a six-letter word while the others still build a five-letter word. This may give everyone a win at one level before moving up.

Log Jammin'

GROUP SIZE:
2 - 4 per jumping area. (Multiple groups can occupy the same pool or pier area.)

TIME:
As long as interest allows

PROPS:
- 15 to 20 midaronis (depending on the height of the jumpers)
- A safe ledge to jump off of into at least three feet of water

OBJECTIVES:
Jump, belly-flop style, onto a bed of noodles and stay afloat.

HISTORY:
The belly flop has been around since living bodies were jumping into water. During our water brainstorming for noodle pool games we added some padding to the flop... or did we?

PREPARATION:
Set out as many noodles as you need, side-by-side in the water to form a "water raft" structure. Make sure this raft is at least two feet from the side of the pool (or pier) heading out perpendicular from the edge. If you have at least one person on each side of the raft putting it together, it goes much faster.

INSTRUCTIONS:
The logjam jumper should be aligned behind the raft of noodles and up out of the water on the edge of the pool or pier. When the jumper is ready he or she says, "Ready to Jam!" The players in the water should back away from the raft a bit to avoid any body-to-body contact with the jumper. The jumper then dives upon the noodle raft to (hopefully) end up afloat. Rotate jumpers and landing pad builders as long as interest allows.

LEADER NOTES:
Please be cautious. Stay clear of edges and shallow bottoms.

You might want to warn the jumpers not to jump too high. This belly flop method doesn't sting as much, but it can knock the wind out of the jumper if he or she is not experienced! Be prepared to help a high-flying human out of the water if he or she does not heed your warning.

VARIATIONS:
Is the "Nestea Plunge" possible? (A back-flop) I think this one might hurt a bit!

Instead of flopping into the water and attempting to stay afloat, try grabbing and holding on to as many floating minironis and meatballs as possible. We call it "Fish In A Barrel." Using a few midaronis, corral the short noodles into an area for the jumper to fall on. The player jumps or falls from the edge of the pool or pier while grabbing all the noodles he can on the way under. Only the noodles trapped by the

jumper on the way down can be counted. The
current record is 14 meatballs.

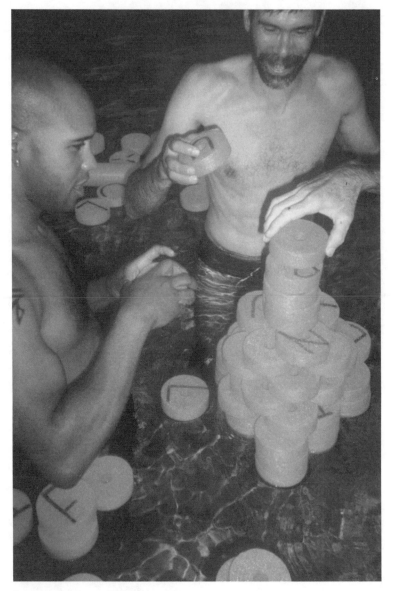

Water Tower

GROUP SIZE:
1 - 4 players for each tower and just as many to "spit foam"

TIME:
10 - 20 minutes

PROPS:
• Dozens of meatballs

OBJECTIVES:
Build a noodle tower that floats on the water.

HISTORY:
Meatballs float very well and they stack very well too. While a group of us were in the pool we started building our own noodle towers for height. We also noticed right away that there is an easy way to propel a meatball besides throwing it.

PREPARATION:
Pour a "bunch" of meatballs in the shallow end of the pool.

SCENARIO:
You have been commissioned to design and build fish food silos. The taller the better. Since the fish can smell the food if too much of it is in the water, you have been asked to minimize the tower's direct exposure to the water. In other words, build it so that it floats on only one meatball if possible.

Unfortunately, there are flying foam fish that may cause you problems during construction.

INSTRUCTIONS:
Stacking team:
Stack meatballs one at a time to build tall towers. As you are building, others will be attempting to topple your tower with flying foam. Feel free to guard your tower. You will have 5 minutes to build.

Foam Spitting Team:
Don't put the meatballs or any water in your mouths. Your job is to topple any towers as the stacking team builds them. You must stay at least 5 feet away from towers. Your resources to topple the

towers are meatballs floating in the pool. If you pinch a meatball between your thumb and index finger, it will pop or "spit" out of your pinch and travel much more than 5 feet. This meatball spit technique is your only way to topple a tower. Work quickly. You only have 5 minutes.

LEADER NOTES:
When the game begins watch the stackers to make sure they are only stacking one meatball at a time and watch the spitters to make sure they are not throwing the meatballs or making waves to topple the towers.

When the 5 minutes have expired, change roles and go for another round.

VARIATIONS:
Simply make this a stacking contest and forget the flying noodles.

Add more noodles to the base and build a floating igloo or a castle. A floating pipe-shaped shelter can be fun to put your head into. It's like your own private space in the pool.

&- Variations -&

Over the years, people have sent us adapted activity
ideas and instructions. The activities in this section
represent some of those variations. Some are based
on activities from the last book and some are noodle
adaptations from popular activities that many people
already facilitate. I know there are more out there
and we have received more than we can print. Keep
the ideas coming!

Elbow Tag Trio

GROUP SIZE:
12 to 36 (or more) players

TIME:
15 to 20 minutes

PROPS:
- 1 Midaroni and 1 meatball for each group of three players in the game
- Boundary markers for the area of play such as cones, tape lines, string line, midaronis

OBJECTIVES:
Be the last team in the playing area with a meatball on the back of a player's hand.

HISTORY:
This is an elongated version of Flippin' Burgers found in the first 50 Ways to Noodle. Rob Benson had a group of 45 people and not enough noodles for

everyone to play in pairs. Out of necessity, he tried this variation with a lot of success.

INSTRUCTIONS:
Set up the boundary area so all the players understand where the boundaries are. Don't make them so big that players have to run a lot. Moving is a little more tricky when people are linked. Break your large group up into groups of three (or four if needed). Give each group one midaroni and one meatball.

Each small team is asked to link together at the elbows into a line. The first player in line will get the midaroni; the last player will start with the meatball. The last player in line will need to place the meatball on the back of her free hand (the one not linked with the other players). The meatball cannot be held on the back of the hand in any way except by gravity – the only thing that can touch the meatball is the back of the hand it is on top of. The lead player of each group will be using the noodle to dislodge the meatball from the tail player of the other teams. Only allow "jabbing" motions with the noodles as opposed to swatting and up and down, motions. This prevents some of the high-speed face contact that might occur.

The idea during play is to protect your meatball and dislodge the meatballs of the other teams. Each team will have three plays. When the meatball falls off a hand to the ground, this is one play. (Notice we said, "to the ground." If the tail player is able to catch the meatball WITH THE FREE HAND before it hits the ground, she can place it back on her hand and continue playing without rotating players.) At that point the small group must stop, rotate positions in line - a new leader and tail player - then return to the game. When the meatball falls to the ground the second time, rotate players then return to the game. When the meatball falls a third time, the entire group moves to the outside of the boundary area to watch the remainder of the game. (If we have players that are playing "nicely" we give them noodles when they come out to the side and they continue the dislodging action from outside of the boundary area.)

Play down to the last two teams with meatballs still atop the hand – two teams can stay away from each other pretty well for a long time. Stop the game if it drags on so that everyone can play again. But hey! If the group wants to go until one team wins, who are we to say otherwise?

LEADER NOTES:
Keep a close eye on swatting noodle motions. If disregarded it could get a little messy – if you know what we mean.

VARIATIONS:
Try this one with overly small boundaries. The game turns a bit more strategic. When we do this variation, we don't allow the dislodging from outside the boundaries option when teams are out of the game.

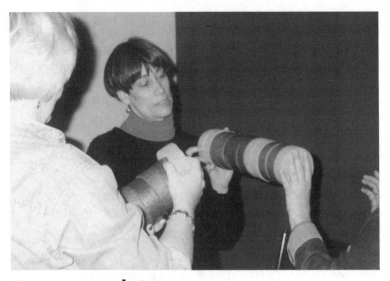

Personal Press

GROUP SIZE:
4 players per press

TIME:
10 - 15 minutes

PROPS:
• Approximately 30 meatballs for each pair

OBJECTIVE:
Pairs of players try to press as many meatballs as possible together horizontally between their hands while revealing information about themselves.

INSTRUCTIONS:
Dump at least 30 meatballs (or more if you have them) in a big pile. Two people will partner and two others will stand so they can help the partners gather meatballs to add to the noodle bridge.

Each player will use one hand as they press, and the other as an adder. Players start by pressing the palms of their press hands together. Then, with the help of the two non-pressers, add one meatball at a time between the pressed hands. As each meatball is added, the player tells his partner and the two helpers something about himself. The information can be anything that helps the four players get acquainted. If the partners want to keep track, they should count the meatballs as they go or ask the helpers to count because if they lose-um, all the meatballs get mixed up with the others on the floor.

LEADER NOTES:
When people have finished pressing, pause and ask the whole group for information they remember. Many times there are some very interesting facts shared.

We like to stress this game as a challenge to the pairs, not a competition between pairs. Go PBs. (Paired Best). As of the writing of this book, 54 meatballs is the longest bridge we have seen.

VARIATIONS:
To add some fun, ask people to start their information sharing with the words, "Oh yea, well...", each time they share something new. The activity quickly takes on the atmosphere of tall tales and sportsman stories.

Identity Crisis

GROUP SIZE:
10 to 30 players

TIME:
30 - 45 minutes

PROPS:
- Masking tape and markers to write names on the tape <u>or</u> noodles with enough letters or numbers on them so that everyone gets a different letter or number
- 1 Meatball or minironi for each person
- Approximately 80 feet of rope for a rope circle boundary
- 1 Bandanna for each person
- 1 Hula-hoop

OBJECTIVE:
Verbally guide someone into an area to blindly retrieve your noodle or theirs.

HISTORY:
Kip Prichard introduced this activity at a state games conference in 1994. We all had a great time playing it. My partner and I decided to place our objects on the far-left side of the hoop so that they would be easy for us to find. It would have worked, too, if it hadn't been for all those other people's objects rolling around in the hoop. I had a hard enough time locating the hoop much less my partner's object!

PREPARATION:
Select a site where there is open space large enough to accommodate your rope circle and a few feet all the way around the rope circle. Place a hula-hoop in the center of the circle of rope. Provide each person in the group with a noodle and a bandanna (a strip of masking tape, and a pen or marker if necessary to make each noodle unique).

INSTRUCTIONS:
Please take hold of the rope and form it into a circle. When it looks good, set it on the ground.

Divide into pairs.

Take a piece of tape and stick it to your meatball, then write your name on the tape. If your noodles are already marked, simply get a noodle and remember the letter or number marked on it.

Place your meatball in the hoop and come back to the outside of the rope circle.

This is a race. Each person should retrieve their partner's meatball or their own. One partner has the resources of sight and speech, but cannot cross the line during the activity unless he is blindfolded; the other can move to the hoop but is blindfolded. The hoop and rope boundary cannot be moved.

Each blind player must safely go to the object pile (no running please), picks up a meatball and displays it to his partner to see if it belongs to either the sighted or blind partner. If it does belong to one of them, the blind partner returns blindly to the outside of the circle with the noodle and the partners exchange roles. If not, he continues to search for the item until he retrieves it.

Noodles must be carried, not thrown or rolled, and a person can only transport one meatball at a time. Please place noodles that are not yours or your partner's back into the hoop.

LEADER NOTES:
In most cases, some noodles are bumped or kicked out of the hula-hoop. Quickly return the misplaced noodles to the hula-hoop.

With a little careful wording you can change this partner activity into a whole team activity. In the team version, a blind person can get a meatball and be guided to its sighted owner. Another way to frame the team challenge is that all the rules in the instructions stay the same except that partners do not have to exchange roles and the timer will stop when everyone has their own meatball and is out of the circle. The challenge then becomes how quickly can all the noodles be recovered and distributed. Groups as large as 30 people can usually complete the task is 35 seconds or less.

Make sure you are in a place where you can be really noisy.

VARIATIONS:
Instead of a rope circle, use a starting line and place the hoop approximately 25 feet away. This version does not require quite as much space, but it may be a little noisier and the timing may be a little slower.

NOTES:

_____

_____

_____

_____

_____

_____

_____

Car Wash

GROUP SIZE:
12 to 20 players

TIME:
15 to 25 minutes

PROPS:
• 1 Midaroni for every player (a midaroni for each
  player's hand if you have enough)

PREPARATION:
Make two lines of people shoulder to shoulder and
the lines approximately four feet apart from each
other.

OBJECTIVE:
Players run through a line of noodles without
slowing down.

HISTORY:
This variation of a trust run comes out of a natural progression of people not hitting each other to people hitting anything that moves!

INSTRUCTIONS:
Give each player a midaroni and ask the group to stand in one of two lines. Have the two lines of players face each other. Players hold the midaroni about stomach high and horizontal to the ground so there is one flat level of noodles when the instructor looks down in-between the lines (the noodles should look like a zipper from a birds-eye view).

From here, the instructor will back up about 15 to 20 feet away from one end of the line (we like to demonstrate this first so the players see that it works -- we hope). Inform the group that you will be running through the middle of the line. Ask the players to try to hit you with their noodle as you pass through the middle. Please keep the hits below the shoulder level and stay in the lines.

The runner gives a primal shout, "READY FOR A CAR WASH?" The lines shout back, "READY." The runner is off in a blaze down the gauntlet of noodles with his arms over his head like a helmet.

With a successful pass, ask who would like to try a run through the noodles. The instructor picks someone and takes her noodle and place in line. "Ready for a car wash," "Ready," "RUN!" Continue the process until everyone has had the opportunity to try.

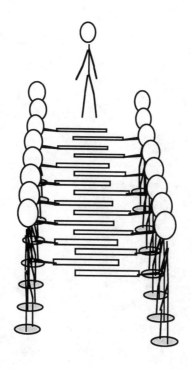

LEADER NOTES:
This activity may be very challenging for some players. It does involve a lot of trust and perceived risk taking.

You might not want to try this activity until the group has a chance to build trust in each other. The activity is a lot of fun. It gives people permission to hit each other with noodles. People tend to laugh a lot. Don't worry about injuries as long as the hits stay below the shoulders and the runners keep their "helmets" on. People will want to take off glasses so that if the glasses fall, they won't be stepped on.

Noodle Doodles 2-dles

GROUP SIZE:
10 to 30 (or more) players

TIME:
15 to 25 minutes

PROPS:
• 1 Midaroni for each player

OBJECTIVES:
Create a variety of designated shapes as quickly as possible. Then, as a team, create a word that represents your group.

HISTORY:
This is a continuation of Noodle Doodles from the first 50 Ways to Noodle. If you are Doodling with your Noodles be sure to share your Doodles for 3-dles.

INSTRUCTIONS:
Split your large group up into small teams of three or four. Make sure each player has a noodle. (Hopefully you won't have to remind them not to beat on each other before, during, and after this one.) Have each group find their own space to work in – not too far away. You will be calling out a shape – a letter, number, or thing – that the small groups will have to make with their noodles. Only the noodles can be used to make the shapes. Here are some examples - a fish, a boat, the letter A, B, H (or whatever), the number 4, 8, 12 (or whatever – be careful not to exceed shape versus noodle allotment).

You will point to a small group and quickly tell them what to make. The rest of the group will start a slow countdown from five. The small group should have their doodle finished by the time the rest of the group gets to zero. Do this with each of the small groups using a different doodle designation each time. Notice we never said this was a competition. We're just working together to meet the objective at hand.

After the small group warm-up, try a slightly higher pressure challenge. Assemble half of the players together for a larger group challenge. Ask this group to (using all the available noodles in their group) form a 5-letter word or picture that represents their purpose for getting together, or something they stand for, or signifies something that is important to all of them, or something they want to strive for, or…(Just pick one, but you get the idea.). Have them create this word or picture so it is on the ground and no player needs to hold any of the noodles. (This is a great photo op. when complete – have the group, "stand behind" their word.) Meanwhile, the other half of the group will start a slow countdown starting with 10. Switch group roles.

If you have time, feel free to join the whole group together to form a shape or set of words that use all the noodles. This time you will start a slow countdown from 15.

LEADER NOTES:
The countdowns are simply a way to increase the intensity of the activity. Decide for yourself if it is appropriate for your group.

This is a great energizer to get everyone up and going. It also emphasizes how small groups are able to work together in demanding situations. You might run into the question, "Do you want the shapes on the ground or should we hold it up?" We will answer, "Yes." (Are we there to give them answers or assist them in finding the answers for themselves?)

Sloshbucklers

GROUP SIZE:
10 to 20 players (even numbers are best for this one)

TIME:
20 to 30 minutes

PROPS:
(Sorry, this one's a bit equipment intensive, but it is WAY fun.)
- 1 Midaroni for each player (you'll need 2 different colored noodles – one color for each team)
- 1 Sturdy plastic cup for each player (Really, these have to be sturdy. The best ones come from the

fast food places for fountain drinks [not that we want you to eat there].) These cups should all be the same size <u>or</u> make sure each player starts out with the same amount of water.
- 1 Container to measure water (We suggest something bigger than a measuring "cup." *That* measures just a cup.)
- A source of water
- Boundary markers

OBJECTIVES:
Be the team with the most water in cups after the "buckling".

HISTORY:
Chris was looking for a fun noodle activity for a school field day. The theme was Medieval times. Running at each other with the long noodles would have been fun, but too hot for the May date in Texas. So, from an inspiration of Flippin' Burgers (in the first 50 Ways to Noodle) he adding a little water to the mix and came up with this one. (Chris wanted to call this one Limp Noodle, you know, water, noodles, "limp noodle?") Well, we went with the present name for political reasons.

PREPARATION:
You will want to setup near a water supply of some sort. We even had to wheel a (clean) garbage can filled with water for one game. A hose, pool, or clean lake work well. Then set up a good size boundary area based on the size of your group.

Keep in mind; players will be getting wet, so attire might need to be considered.

SCENARIO:
The clash between desert pirate crews can be brutal. You will have to combine all the skills your mates can muster. You and you fellow pirates have encountered another crew on the high dunes. Go after their most valuable resource... water. The crew with the most water in the end will win.

INSTRUCTIONS:

Ready? Split your group in half. If the teams end up uneven you can divvy out the water so both teams have the same at the start of the game. Give each player a midaroni – each team should have a different colored noodle. Then each player should get a cup. If all the cups are the same size, each player can fill his own cup with water – all the way to the top. If the cups are different sizes, you will need to fill each cup with water using the measuring container – for a good game have each cup filled with at least one and a half to two cups of water. (If there are an uneven number of players on one side, let's say six on one side seven on the other. Fill up 6 players on each team so they have the same amount of water, then have the team with seven players share some water with the seventh player – all players on the team with seven players should start out with the same amount of water.

Okay, here is the objective. Players will be holding a noodle in one hand and the cup of water in the other – the cup cannot be held against the body. We have seen players hold the cup from underneath, from the top, and around the middle. When the game begins, each team has one minute to slosh out the water from the cups of the other team. This is done by trying to hit the cups or arms of the players holding cups and make them spill the water. When the minute is up, the referee (facilitator) will measure out the remaining water of each team. The most water wins the round. You can only remain in the game if you have water in your cup (at least a tablespoon). If a player has all of his water sloshbuckled out he must move to the side of the boundary area to watch the rest of the match (or players who go to the side could be "sideliners" - see, See Foam, Tag). If a player stays in the game and cannot produce more than a tablespoon for the referee, his team forfeits the round.

LEADER NOTES:

Make sure the players understand that sloshbuckling (contact) should be intended for the cup and the arm attached to the cup. Other body contact should be avoided. There will be other "unintentional" contact to be expected, but monitor the action so the "intentional" body sloshing is noticed and dealt with.

NOTES:

_____

_____

_____

_____

_____

_____

_____

Fortune Seekers

GROUP SIZE:
16 to 28 players

TIME:
20 to 30 minutes

PROPS:
• 4 Midaronis

- Many meatballs – 75 to 100. The 98 meatballs in the standard letter set (as described in Letter Opener) will work great.
- If you have hula-hoops you can use one for every four players, or any type of container to hold the meatballs that the players will be collecting.

OBJECTIVES:
Collect as many meatballs as possible within the time allowed.

HISTORY:
Chris developed this activity to meet the needs of his elementary physical education classes. Treasure Seekers is a less complicated version of Gold Digger found in the first 50 Ways to Noodle book.

PREPARATION:
The best area to play this one is in a gym that will have a center court jump circle. However, this jump circle is not necessary to reach F^3 (the full fun factor). Place all the meatballs you have in a big pile in the center of the playing area – the center court jump circle if you have one. Set the 4 midaronis near the pile of meatballs. Place the hula-hoops or other containers at least 20 to 25 feet from the pile of meatballs. You will want one hula-hoop for every three or four players in your group. Set the hoops equidistant apart from each other so that they end up forming a circle around the pile of meatballs.

SCENARIO:
You are all followers of the great Bilbow Baggins (Lord of the Rings scenario). You, the treasure hunters, have come to the lair of the dragons to seek your fortune. Each small group has set up a base camp at a safe distance from the dragons. Your task now is to sneak by the dragons and collect the treasures you came for. Enter the lair with caution to avoid the singeing flame of the dragon's breadth.

INSTRUCTIONS:
Divide your group into small groups of three or four

players and ask each small group to sit behind one of the hoops or containers.

Choose one small team to be the first "dragons." Ask them to come out into the middle. Give each of the dragons a midaroni. Here's how it plays. One player from each small team is allowed to go for a piece of treasure. The remainder of each team will be sitting behind their base camp hoop – safe from the dragons. The dragons can move anywhere between the treasure and the hoops. The dragons do not move beyond the circle of hoops. The dragons will be preventing the treasure hunters from stealing the treasure by tagging the hunters with the noodle (their breath-of-flames). Any hunter that is tagged (singed) must return to his base camp for first aid. The next player in line from that team can then enter the lair to try to obtain some treasure. If a treasure hunter reaches the pile of treasure he can pick up one piece (Each piece is much too heavy to carry more than one.), then try to return to safety unsinged. If he reaches the outer limit of the hoops, the treasure hunter can place his bounty into his hoop (or other container). If the hunter is tagged after obtaining a piece of treasure and before reaching safety, he must set down the treasure where he was tagged and then return to his base camp for first aid. Then the next player in line can enter the lair.

Since dragons have limited use of their small hands, they cannot pick up any treasure to return it to the pile. So, all treasure stays where it is set until another treasure hunter can come to pick it up.

A little strategy in this game goes a long way. Each round lasts for 3 minutes. We go around to determine who has the most treasure. The team with the most treasure becomes the new dragon team. If this team has already been dragons, they pick a group who hasn't been the dragons to go protect the treasure.

LEADER NOTES:
A couple of heads up here: 1) There are ample opportunities for students to come in contact with each other in an abrupt manner. It is important for the players in your group to have the body and spatial awareness needed for this activity. 2) Even though it is innovative, we do not allow the kamikaze maneuver – one player diving into the pile of treasure to spread it out for others to collect (This is actually really fun to do, but adds little to this game.). If this were to happen, stop the game, redo the pile of treasure, and ask that this not to happen again. Thanks. 3) To slow things down a bit, require the dragons to have both hands on their noodle at all times.

A big also. We hope you have time for each team to be the dragons. It tends to be a large downer when groups don't "get their turn."

VARIATIONS:
An interesting thought we had while writing this one. What if, after the 3 minutes is up, each group, even the dragons, were to make up as many words with their treasure as they could (dragons would hopefully have some treasure left to work with) – like in the activity, Word Builder. Then you could count each piece of treasure as a point and each word for points – 2 letter word 2 points, three letter word 3 points and so on. How about that for some added academics? (Let us know how this works.)

Smack Down

Smack Down

GROUP SIZE:
8 to 15 players

TIME:
10 to 15 minutes

PROPS:
- 1 Midaroni for each player
- A good floor to smack the noodle on – sorry, grass isn't the best place for this one.

OBJECTIVES:
Count (or "Smack" seems to be more appropriate) up to the number of players without two players counting/smacking at the same time.

HISTORY:
This is a prop variation to the classic Karl Rohnke Count Down activity. Using the noodles adds a bit more sound and commitment to the process.

INSTRUCTIONS:
Each player will have his own noodle. Do some practice smacking on the floor to find your sound. (Now this can, no let us restate, this <u>will</u> be loud. So if you are not into loud or you are not in a place to be loud, then pass on this one.) Once each player has found his sound, give the instructions. Your objective is to smack the floor for to the number of players in your group. If you have twelve players you are going for twelve smacks. Each player can only smack one time on the way up to twelve. If two players smack at the same time, you all have to start over. This is all done with your eyes closed. No preplanning and, in the spirit of adventure, no smacking around in a circle – too easy, no fun!

LEADER NOTES:
You will want a monitor for the process. We usually choose ourselves to do so. The monitor will keep

count aloud. If two smacks go down at once, the monitor will state, "Restart!" and then start counting again from 1.

And, if you really like the noise you can create with the noodles, check out Noodle Drumming.

VARIATIONS:
The original Count Down is set up the same way but players call out the numbers until they count down to the number one. If two numbers are called at the same time, the group starts over.

Ask the group to sit in a circle facing outward.

NOTES:

_____

_____

_____

_____

_____

_____

_____

See Foam, Tag

GROUP SIZE:
15 to 30 players

TIME:
15 to 20 minutes

PROPS:
- 1 Midaroni for each player – every third of the group should have a different colored noodle (so you need three colors of noodles).
- Boundary markers to designate the playing area such as rope so you don't lose anyone down the block.

OBJECTIVES:
Be the last player from your team to be in the playing area.

HISTORY:
This one is a spin-off of Partner Tag found in the first 50 Ways to Noodle. We added a bit more team tagging to the adventure with a measurable ending for those who want to know, "Who wins?" (But hey, we all win if we play, right?!)

PREPARATION:
Set up the boundary area large enough for the size of your group, you can adjust it during play if needed. Make the space large enough for players to move around safely, but not too large that the players will tire too quickly.

INSTRUCTIONS:
Gather in the boundary area. Split your group up into three even teams and give each player on each team the same color of noodle – each team has a different color. Ask the oldest player on each team to be IT first. The three ITs stand in the middle of their boundary, hold up their noodles and say, "I am IT for the _____ (each state the color of their teams noodles) team!" At the same time, all the other players are going to be moving as far away from their IT as possible – within the boundary area. After the "noodle call" the ITs go off to tag one of the players, below the waist, on their team – signified by the fact that they are holding the same colored

noodle as the IT tagger. So, the idea here is that there are three different tag games going on at one time.

When a new player is tagged, below the waist, this person stands still, holds up her noodle and claims (loudly), "I am IT for the Yellow (or whatever color) team." Then moves off to find another player on her team to tag. This process continues for 45 seconds. The player who is IT when the time is up (Blow a whistle to end the round.), becomes a "Sideliner" for the remainder of the game (explained more below).

For the next round choose the oldest player from each team to start as IT again. Play the same game with one added feature. The Sideliners can also tag players from their team, below the waist. The Sideliners must stay outside the boundary area for their tag to be counted (Having lines on the floor or ground is especially helpful for this.). When a player gets tagged by a Sideliner, he holds up his noodle and claims (very loudly), "I am IT for the Red team." The player that was IT for the red team is now un-IT and joins the fleeing crowd of Red noodle players. Now, there is a chance that two (or more) players might be IT at the end of the round, if this happens the oldest player who is IT will become a Sideliner. Then start the next round as before.

The end of the game will find a showdown between two team members of each team. Lots of strategies here. The final, or winner, will be the player who is not IT when the whistle blows.

LEADER NOTES:
It will be up to you, and the maturity of the group, if you want to allow "blocking." Players would be allowed to block the IT from tagging them using their noodle – as they might do in fencing. However, be warned, this produces lots of flailing noodles – and if you've noodled before, you know what this looks like. More often than not, we do not allow blocks. The noodle can only be used as a tagging resource.

VARIATIONS:
If a Sideliner tags a team member, this player tagged comes out to the side to join the Sideliners while the Sidliner reenters the action as IT for his team.

NOTES:

_____

_____

_____

_____

_____

_____

Team Noodle Steal

GROUP SIZE:
10 to 50 players (or more if you have a loud voice)

TIME:
15 to 20 minutes

PROPS:
- 2 Midaronis for every 10 players
- 4 Cones for each game if you have some. You can use them to mark the starting line.

OBJECTIVES:
Steal the noodle and pass it to all your teammates faster than the other team.

HISTORY:
You remember the dreaded, "steal the bacon" activity you played as a child. All the fast kids loved this game. And if you were not that fast, you would rather be in wrestling (or not). Anyway, this came about in a pinch with a gigantic group that turned out to be lots of fun. So, why not?

INSTRUCTIONS:
Divide your large group so that you will have even teams of five or six players. Two teams will be playing head to head with each other. So, if you have 20 players, make four teams of five. Two teams will be playing against each other, so you will have two games going on at once. (You can work out whatever numbers work best for your group based on how the game is played.)

Set up two teams across from each other, like the old steal the bacon scenario. You will want about 10 to 15 feet between teams. Having some cones to mark the starting lines helps in the fairness of the operation. Place 2 midaronis, a different color for each team between the two groups – a fair distance between the two. Number off each team of players from 1 to 5 (or whatever number you have). Players will keep this number throughout the entire game. You are ready to play.

When you call out a number, that player must run out to get the team's noodle, bring it back to one end of his line. The noodle must then be passed down the line of players, each player obtaining and then passing the noodle to the next player (no skipping players) until the last person in line gets it and holds the noodle up. The first team to hold the noodle up gets the point. Return the noodles to the center for the next round. We will play to 10, win by two.

LEADER NOTES:

This activity may take on some problem solving and team discussions (that might not have anything to do with problem solving). So let them run with it if time allows. If you have more than one game going on at once, you can change the teams after a game is won.

We always ask the leaders that we train to teach their groups how to play within the spirit of compassion or what we like to call Coopetition – playing competitively while supporting the efforts of all players. Please keep this in mind and monitor the actions and communication of your groups.

VARIATIONS:

Use those math formulas to get to numbers – 2 + 3, 5697 – 5694, the square root of 9, and so on.

You can also play one game with three or four teams at once – form up in a triangle or square and just have enough noodles in the center of the shape for each team.

Instead of holding up the noodle to indicate a finish, smack it on the floor.

:) Just For Fun (:

This section contains activities that are not intended to teach anything in particular. They are not so structured that you arrive at the end or necessarily find a winner or loser. These activities are intended to just play for the sheer fun of it. At a recent conference we presented four people the Noodle Loop The Loop in an open space on the exhibit showroom. Forty -five minutes later there were twenty laughing, sweating people playing as hard as they could. Why did they do it? It was "just for fun!"

What You Really Want To Do

GROUP SIZE:
Any

TIME:
15 Seconds

PROPS:
• 1 Midaroni for each person

OBJECTIVES:
Hit people with your noodle.

HISTORY:
This activity has been a long running joke and psychological thriller since Chris and I facilitated the first Noodle activities several years ago. The joke is that we never give any specific instructions to the group, but they always know what to do. The psychological thriller is to observe people's restraint not to do "what they really want to do" until you finally give them permission at the end of the day or just before a break. Why do people need to hit each other with noodles? I think it must be like gravity -

It's the law!

PREPARATION:
Let people know just before you distribute the noodles that they should avoid doing what they really want to do, because you all will be doing that later.

INSTRUCTIONS:
It is the time you have been waiting for. We have these noodles and it is time to do "What You Really Want To Do." You have 15 seconds; just keep it below the shoulders... GO!

Blow a whistle or use an attention getter when the time has expired.

LEADER NOTES:
Please join in on the action. Sometimes, you might even be the first to whack someone on the knees!

For some younger groups you may want to extend the time of the activity to about a minute to burn off some of that energy they often seem to have.

Horizontal Noodle Running

GROUP SIZE:
Solo Activity (small groups can take turns)

TIME:
5 to 15 minutes

PROPS:
• 1 Midaroni per runner

OBJECTIVES:
To see how long a player can keep a noodle in the horizontal position pressed to the palm of the hand by the pressure of forward motion.

PREPARATION:
You'll need a nice long area to run for this one.

INSTRUCTIONS:
Players will start at the end of a long runway. Grasp the midaroni at the end – palm should be flat against the end as fingers grasp up around the sides. Hold the noodle horizontal to the ground, then, run as fast as possible. The idea will be to move fast enough so the runner can open the fingers so the noodle stays pressed against the palm of the hand by the sheer speed of the runner. The runner will most likely have to try and "right" the noodle while running to keep it on the hand – this takes some practice.

LEADER NOTES:
We haven't really developed a good way to measure how long one can keep the noodle pressed against the hand. However, we have been very successful at burning lots of energy in the process – kids love to burn energy!

VARIATIONS:
On a hot summer day, try this idea with a full glass of water on your forehead!?

Noodle Loop The Loop

GROUP SIZE:
Any

TIME:
10 - 30 minutes

PROPS:
- A minimum of 3 midaronis. Ideally you want a midaroni for each person and half as many noodles as people that can be airborne at any given time. Any midaronis will work; however, the noodles that are hexagonal, star, or flower shaped do the most dramatic loop the loops.

OBJECTIVES:
Push and spin a noodle using another noodle so that it travels through the air in a loop the loop flight. It's a lot of fun!

HISTORY:
This activity is the reward for staying curious. Playing with the noodles can lead to unexpected surprises.

To learn more about why the noodle does a loop the loop, I would suggest researching the Magnus Effect, Bernoulli Effect, and Bjerknes' Tube.

PREPARATION:
Clear a room of fragile items and drinks that could be knocked over. High ceilings are ideal if you do this indoors and calm winds are ideal if you do this activity outdoors.

INSTRUCTIONS:
Hold a midaroni vertically like a tennis racket in your dominant hand and hold another midaroni horizontally to make a cross. Serve the horizontal noodle by letting go, pushing and spinning it with the vertical noodle. I call this serve, "zipping" it because the horizontal noodle makes a zipping sound as it rolls from the bottom end of the vertical noodle to the top. Try it a few times until you get the "feel" of it. It does not take a lot of force to "zip" a noodle and send it 20 or 30 feet. The great thing about the flight is that it tends to do a loop the loop pattern or

the noodle travels an extended time horizontally across the room. Get everyone involved in zipping noodles back and forth.

The instructions above will cause the horizontal noodle to travel up and away from you. If you hold the vertical noodle pointing down, place the horizontal noodle on top near your dominant hand to form a T, and zip the horizontal noodle toward the ceiling, it will loop out and back towards you like a boomerang. With practice this method can be a lot of fun for an individual player.

LEADER NOTES:
Demonstrate the first loop the loop with a noodle and then invite everyone to join you. Once you have shown them and explain that the horizontal noodle needs to spin, people "get it" quickly.

VARIATIONS:
See how long a group can keep one or more noodles in the air by "zipping" them back and forth.

Try using two noodles to catch the flying noodle, then try to send it without touching it with your hands. It's harder than it sounds.

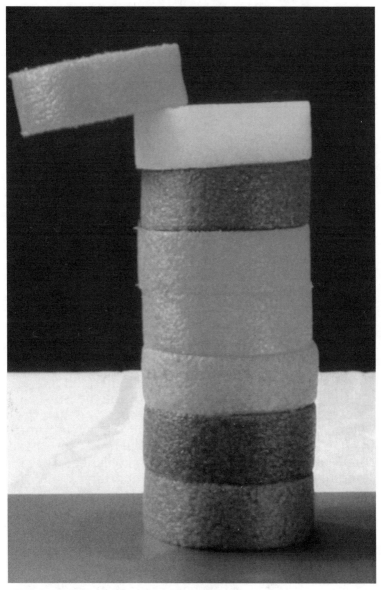

Meatball Sinkers

Meatball Sinkers

GROUP SIZE:
2-10

TIME:
5-15 minutes

PROPS:
• Meatballs and minironis
• Lead weights such as fishing sinkers

OBJECTIVE:
Create the illusion that a meatball is defying gravity.

HISTORY:
The activity called Three Towers in the first noodle book involves stacking meatballs or minironis so that they do not fall. I added this devious twist just to make other players nervous while I played.

PREPARATION:
To make a weighted meatball, take a sharp knife and carefully make a slit into the edge of the meatball a little deeper than the weight, but narrower than the weight. The idea is to be able to hide the weight into an edge of the meatball so that it will not easily fall out. Make as many as you think you will need. Remember that the heavier the weight and the closer to the outside edge it is placed, the more dramatic the results.

SCENARIO:
You and others are attempting to win a huge contract to build Hollywood sets for an upcoming motion picture based on the stories of Dr. Seuss. Part of your job will be to build enormous towers with unusual architecture. Feel free to be creative, but realize that you are being evaluated on your ability to build a tall tower with an unusual design and not allow any of your pieces to fall. If any part of the tower falls during your turn, you might as well

look for another job.

INSTRUCTIONS:
Take turns stacking meatballs and minironis to build a tall tower. Feel free to take construction risks as you build.

LEADER NOTES:
Reserve for yourself some weighted meatballs to place on the tower. Enjoy the facial expressions of other players as you carefully place a meatball in a gravity defying position. Others will undoubtedly try to follow your lead and do the same thing. Of course they will not be able to duplicate your feats and the tower, or at least their piece, will usually fall.

The weighted meatballs should never be used to hit or throw hard since the weights can come out of the meatball and fly at injuring speeds.

VARIATIONS:
Roll the weighted meatball across the floor. It is harder to catch than your average noodle. If you are careful not to throw the meatball hard, try tossing the weighted meatball like a Frisbee.

Have You Ever Noodled?...

GROUP SIZE:
10 to 30+ players

TIME:
10 to 15 minutes

PROPS:
- 1 Midaroni for every two players
- A good whistle if you have one

OBJECTIVES:
Smack other players (safely) with the midaronis as much as possible in the allowed amount of time. And have fun doing so darn it!

HISTORY:

The first list of "Have You Evers" by Karl Rohnke that I saw was in the 1988 book *The Bottomless Bag* - put into book form after several years as a newsletter. So, the idea has been around for some time. The first game version (that I know of) came out in Karl's *Bottomless Baggie* in 1991, "Have You Ever - Circle Game." We add a bit of extra action to our version - definitely not for the meek.

INSTRUCTIONS:

Circle up all the players in an open area. Each player should have a little elbowroom. Place all the midaronis in the center of the group in a nice big pile. Then ask the group a question like, "Have you ever put more than four pieces of bubble gum in your mouth at one time?" Now, if any player in the group has done that, they would go into the middle of the circle, grab a noodle and start whacking the other gum chewers who came into the circle. (Now, if a player has in fact stuck more than four pieces of gum in their mouth but does not want to get pounded by noodle whackers, this is okay - pounding by choice - they can choose to stay where they are and watch the carnage.) After about 15 seconds, blow the whistle (or yell "FREEZE") loudly. This will indicate to the players to put down the noodles and return to a place in the ring of players. As the facilitator, you can ask the questions or you can choose others in the group that can ask questions. Depending on the group, you might have to give out an appropriate rating for the questions - G, PG (We would never go beyond PG!?)

LEADER NOTES:

Be aware of the energy level of your group before playing this one. If you think everyone will stay respectful and appropriate during the game, it is loads of fun. You know what could happen if the group is not ready!?

VARIATIONS:
The recent twists on the questions are, "Have you never?" and "Would you like to?"

NOTES:

_____

_____

_____

_____

_____

_____

Noodle Birds

Noodle Birds

GROUP SIZE:
1 to 6 players per bird

TIME:
10 to 15 minutes

PROPS:
- 1 Minironi-sized noodle piece
- 3 Large feathers (found in a variety of colors at most of those big craft stores)
- Glue (optional)

OBJECTIVES:
Keep the Noodle Bird in the air as long as possible.

HISTORY:
(As much as we know without looking.) The Pateka has been around for a long time, coming from South America (we think). It is a leather foot-bag with feathers sticking out one of the ends. Recently, Dr. Jim Cain has been sharing a variation called the Funderbird who he credits to Bill Henderson (You can find more on the Funderbirds in Dr. Cain's book, *Teamwork & Teamplay.*). Well, the story goes on! Our friend Mike Spiller, with his wonderful curiosity, stuck some feathers into a minironi, and the Noodle Bird was created. Then (if that wasn't enough), we added Sam's sinker idea (found in this section) to give the birds a bit more spunk.

PREPARATION:
Here's how we do it. So far the optimal noodle piece is a 3 to 5 inch section cut from a maxaroni or midaroni (We haven't tried the maxaroni rex size yet.). Then, you'll need 3 long feathers; at least 8 inches from tip to tip, for each bird. For the spunk in the bird pick up 3 or 4 washers, about the size and weight of a quarter. Ready to build. Take the feathers and press the sharp quill ends into the center of one of the ends of the noodle. Place the

feathers so the bow of the feather is away from the others (see picture). Then, make three or four small cuts, with a sharp knife, on the same end as the feathers, just large enough for the washers to be pressed into – again, the cuts are on the same end as the feathers. DO NOT make the cuts into the side of the noodle or the bottom – washers will fly like shrapnel if they are placed anywhere else (we've done extensive, painful, testing on this, take our word for it!!) Where were we? Okay, place the washers in the cuts so you cannot see the washer sticking out from the top. As an added security, feel free to glue the washers into the noodle. Ready to play?!

SCENARIO:

Deep in the jungles of Peru lives a small, unusual bird called a Pateka. It has only three feathers and does more hopping than flying. Although water does not harm the bird, it does keep it on the ground where predators can see its brightly colored markings. Adults native to the region where the bird lives care for the small animal by knocking off the water that has soaked into its soft skin. To do this, they pick up the soaked bird and pat it up into the air so that another person can pat it into the air again. Eventually the water will have been knocked off enough for the Pateka to fly away. So if you ever see kids playing with a feathered toy, patting it into the air to someone else, you can be sure they are practicing for the day they too can take care of the unusual Pateka.

INSTRUCTIONS:

There are several ways to use the Noodle Bird. One of the easiest is just gathering your group together, then hitting the Bird around to see how long you can keep a volley going or how many times the group can hit it before the Bird lands on the ground – count each hit as you go. No player is allowed to hit the Bird twice in a row. Most hits are done with an underhand motion, like a serve in volleyball. There might be some overhand hits in there to save the Bird from landing. Dr. Cain likes to make a name game out of the hits – every time a player hits the bird, he or she calls out their own name. After some time at this, every time the Bird is hit, the hitting player has to call the name of another player in the group – the bird does not have to go to this player.

LEADER NOTES:
If you want to understand more about the spunk, try the Noodle Bird without the washers in it. Then add one washer and try it again. Add a second washer and try again, and so on. You should be able to tell the difference in the loft. Then you can adjust it for different situations if needed.

VARIATIONS:
As an initiative activity, have the group see how far they can get the Bird from an initial starting spot. Each player can hit the Bird one time. When the Bird hits the ground, mark the spot. Have another go to see if the group can get the Bird passed that initial spot. How far can they reach with a little practice and by working together?

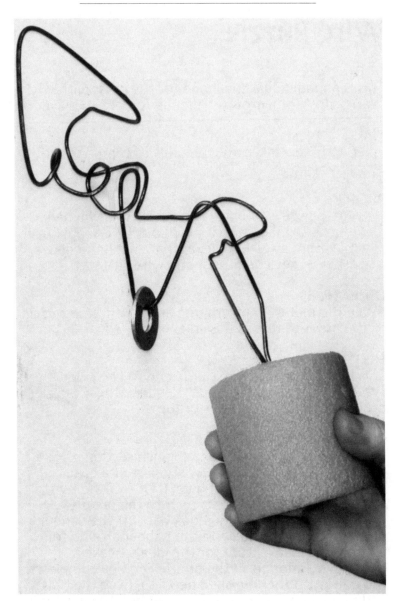

Wire Puzzle

Wire Puzzle

GROUP SIZE:
This is an individual challenge for the most part. See "Variations" for a group challenge for 5 to 10 players.

TIME:
Filler activity – takes only seconds to complete the puzzle

PROPS:
- 1 Wire puzzle - To make the puzzle you will need a wire coat hanger, a 3 to 5 inch piece of noodle from a maxaroni-sized noodle, a small metal ring like a washer or key chain ring, and wire cutters.

OBJECTIVES:
Move the metal ring from one end of the wire puzzle to the other as fast as possible.

HISTORY:
This is another one from our friend Mike Spiller. (We're sure he never sleeps!) He uses these puzzles during down time with his groups.

PREPARATION:
To make the puzzle, get a 3 to 5 inch section of noodle. Then unwind the twisty part of a coat hanger – don't cut anything yet! One of the twisty ends will be used to corkscrew into the noodle. At this point you can cut the hook part off the hanger. Then, be creative and bend the hanger around for your puzzle (see picture for the idea). Make it challenging enough so the puzzle can't be completed too quickly. When finished bending, have the twisty end ready and make sure the other end has a good 2 to 3 inch straight section to pierce into the noodle. Now, first turn the twisty end or the wire into the noodle, just off-center on one of the noodle ends – all the way until the twisty part in concealed. Then, before poking the second wire end into the noodle, put the washer or ring on the wire. Pierce the

straight end into the noodle leaving enough room for the ring you have to lay flat on the noodle piece. Your puzzle is ready.

SCENARIO:
In the days before the first abacus, counting was difficult and higher mathematics was practically impossible. Counting was even a chore. Use the single-beaded abacus to count to five as quickly as possible. You will have to send the ring or bead from one end of the wire to the other five times.

INSTRUCTIONS:
Challenge players to move the ring from one side of the wire to the other. Time each turn to see who can move the ring the fastest.

LEADER NOTES:
If you have time, glue the wire into the noodle for extra strength.

VARIATIONS:
You could create a little team initiative by circling up 5 to 10 players. On "GO" (the time starts) the first player moves the ring to the other side of the wire then passes the puzzle to the next player. This player moves the ring back to the other side of the wire and then passes the puzzle. The next player moves the ring and so on around the circle until the anchor player finishes. Time stops. Can the group beat this first time with another try?

To make the game more difficult, use a washer with a small hole or use a wooden bead.

Ask players to try it with their eyes closed.

Try this one while only looking at the puzzle in the mirror.

Top Secret
Puzzle Solutions

Squares

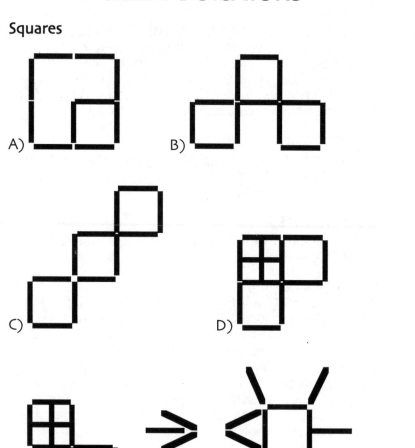

A)

B)

C)

D)

E)

F)

He ducks

Meatball Puzzle Solutions

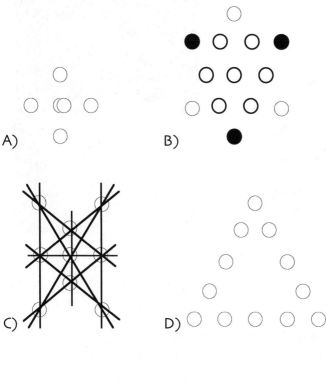

A)

B)

C)

D)

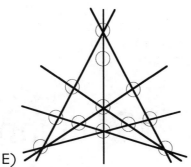

E)

Chris Cavert

Chris has been working and playing in the Human Services field since 1979. He received his undergraduate degree in Physical Education and his Masters Degree in Experiential Education. Chris is a nationally know speaker in the area of Adventure Based Activity Programming that can support pro-social interaction and educational enrichment.

His other published works include the, *E.A.G.E.R. Curriculum: Experiential Activities, Games, and Educational Recreation* * *Games (and other stuff) for Group* books 1 & 2 * *Games (and other stuff) for Teachers* * *Affordable Portables: A Working-Book of Initiative Activities & Problem Solving Elements.* and *Ricochet' and other fun games with an odd ball.*

For additional information on workshops, publications and products visit Chris' web site: www.FUNdoing.com or e-mailing chris@fundoing.com

Sam Sikes

Sam is the founder of DoingWorks, Inc. in Texas, a training organization that specializes in experiential learning techniques.

Sam trains, facilitates, and speaks nationwide in a variety of corporate and educational settings including Fortune 500 companies, small businesses and universities. Best known for his creativity, Sam has trained groups of as few as two people and as many as three thousand. He trains challenge course facilitators, corporate trainers and develops related indoor and outdoor training activities for adults. He is active in organizations such as the Association for Experiential Education and the American Society for Training and Development. In 2000, Sam received the "Karl Rohnke Creativity Award" from the Association for Experiential Education.

Sam holds a Master's Degree in Industrial/Organizational Psychology from the University of Tulsa, and a Bachelor's Degree in Psychology from Texas Tech University in Lubbock.

His published materials include:
Feeding the Zircon Gorilla ⁕ *Executive Marbles* ⁕ *Raptor* ⁕ *50 Ways To Use Your Noodle* ⁕ *Virtual World* ⁕ *Equestrian Knights of Uma* ⁕ 99 of the Best Corporate Games we know!

For more details regarding books, "learnshops", and simulations, contact
Sam at www.DoingWorks.com or (512) 778-6640 or
e-mail- Sam@DoingWorks.com

Additional Contributors

We want to thank these special people for their contributions to this book and their contributions to the world at large.

Karl Rohnke is one of the most widely known Adventure Activity writers in the field of Experiential Education. His generous sharing touches players of all ages and from all over the globe. For more information about Karl's publications, contact Kendall/Hunt at 1-800-228-0810 or contact him directly at www.high5adventure.org

Mike Spiller began Games Of The World in Hawaii in 1984. Today he has collected over 5000 interactive games from his travels to over 21 countries. Mike hosts a Treasure Chest of Ideas Conference and a Clown Circus Camp annually. He has concentrated most recently on traditional Native American games and European Pub games. For workshop information, contact Mike at Rt 3 Box 82A, Giddings, TX 78942 (409) 542-5902.

Dr. Jim Cain is the author of the award winning adventure-based text *Teamwork & Teamplay*, that received the Karl Rohnke Creativity Award presented by the Association for Experiential Education in 1999. He is the Executive Director of the Association for Challenge Course Technology, and manager of the Cornell University Corporate Teambuilding Program For more information contact Jim at, 468 Salmon Creek Road, Brockport, NY 14420, (716) 637-0328, fax- (716) 637-5277
E-mail- teamplay@frontiernet.net

How to Contribute to Future Books

Do you have new
Games?
Problem-Solving Activities?
Pictures?

Send information to:
"More Noodles Book"
DoingWorks
351 County Road 277
Liberty Hill, TX 78642

-or-

Contact us by:
phone- (512) 778-6640
fax- (512) 778-6640
e-mail- Sam@DoingWorks.com
Chris@FUNdoing.com

Ordering more books and supplies . . .

To order additional books and other tools for experiential facilitation and training
contact:

Learning Unlimited Corporation
5155 East 51st Street, Suite 108
Tulsa, OK 74135
(888) 622-4203 toll free
(918) 622-3292
(918) 622-4203 fax
www.LearningUnlimited.com

Need Noodles?

We can send you all the noodles you need or refer you to someone who can. Just contact us and we can provide noodles already cut and bagged.

we accept
MasterCard, Visa, & American Express